The
PRACTICE
OF
PSYCHOTHERAPY
-
Wizardry or Reality?

A look at the field to
see if it's a fit for YOU.

Jim Gordon, Ph.D, MFT
Psychotherapist and Life Coach
Beverly Hills, CA

Welcome! The purpose of this book is to review and gain an introductory understanding of the Practice of Psychotherapy, whether those skills are going to be used in 'counseling', 'psychotherapy', 'therapy', 'life coaching', or just for personal growth. We will learn to understand that the therapist's and counselor's pills are WORDS, and how to learn to use the right ones.

BHCounseling.Com
DrGLifecoach.com

Jim Gordon, Ph.D., MFT #12651
204 S. Beverly Drive, #116
Beverly Hills, CA 90212
BHCounseling@gmail.com
310 271 3784
2nd Edition© 2012

****

Dear Readers,

Congratulations on being interested in the field of PSYCHOTHERAPY and COUNSELING. In reading through this book, I hope you will gain an introductory understanding of the Practice of Psychotherapy whether you will be going into counseling, psychotherapy, therapy, life coaching, or just for your own personal growth. Included is a very brief overview of the principal theories in use today by psychotherapists in the field, but most of the book is aimed at you and your personal growth as you aim for your career.

We will compare theories a bit, and schools of therapy to see if there is one 'magic bullet' that solves all problems, and for you to understand that the therapist's and counselor's pill's are WORDS, and how to learn to use the right ones. In reviewing the material, hopefully, you will get to understand some of the strengths and weaknesses of psychotherapy and realize how much your personality, drive and interest really make it work.

I hope you will look at your own skills and aptitudes before you go into the field of therapy as you complete some of the exercises. You can only be a good therapist, if you understand yourself too! I've written this book based on the experiences in my practice, and pulled info to share that is pertinent.

Throughout the book are some question and answer sections, where you will probe your thoughts and ideas. These questions are there for you to push your growth. Good luck on your journey.

Sincerely,

Dr. G.

****

TABLE OF CONTENTS

Foreword

SECTION I - BASICS

SECTION II - THEORIES OVERVIEW

SECTION III - THERAPISTS BASICS

SECTION IV - FEELINGS -
DEALING WITH THEM

SECTION V - SAMPLING OF DISORDERS

SECTION VI - ISSUES

SECTION VII -
KNOW YOUR DREAMS & FOLLOW YOUR PASSIONS

SECTION VIII - GETTING TO KNOW YOUR CLIENT

APPENDIX

SECTION I
BASICS

RISK

TO LAUGH,
> IS TO RISK APPEARING THE FOOL.

TO WEEP,
> IS TO RISK APPEARING SENTIMENTAL.

TO REACH OUT FOR ANOTHER,
> IS TO RISK INVOLVEMENT.

TO EXPOSE FEELINGS,
> IS TO RISK EXPOSING YOUR TRUE SELF.

TO PLACE YOUR IDEAS, YOUR DREAMS BEFORE
> THE CROWD, IS TO RISK LOSS.

TO LOVE,
> IS TO RISK NOT BEING LOVED IN RETURN.

TO LIVE IS TO RISK DYING,
> TO HOPE IS TO RISK DESPAIR,
>> TO TRY AT ALL IS TO RISK FAILURE,
>>> BUT TO RISK WE MUST -

BECAUSE THE GREATEST HAZARD IN LIFE
> IS TO RISK NOTHING.

THE MAN, THE WOMAN, WHO RISKS NOTHING,
> DOES NOTHING, HAS NOTHING, IS NOTHING.

Are you ready for this field?

Here are many thought questions for you to reflect on before you choose this field. Some are specific and some general, but all pertain to you being "ready for your close-up", in Hollywood terms.

Self-Inventory Reflection Questions

For Multiple choice questions, circle answer, but be prepared to justify your answer. For other questions, not just YES or NO, but clarify you answers.

PART ONE

1. I think the purpose of counseling and psychotherapy is to:
    A. Assist clients in creating solutions to their problems.
    B. Tell others how best to run their life.
    C. Make clients happy and contented.
    D. Always provide an answer or solution to the client's problems.

2. I think that clients who seek out counseling are:
    A. able to find creative solutions on their own.
    B. generally in need of advice on how to proceed to find those solutions.
    C. unable to have progress unless I am very active and assertive.
    D. generally resistant to any change without my help.

3. Counseling and therapy should focus primarily on:
    A. Changing behavior.
    B. Providing insight.
    C. Changing attitudes and feelings.
    D. Challenging values

4. Whose responsibility is it for selecting the goals of counseling?
    A. Primarily the clients.
    B. Primarily the therapist.
    C. A collaborative venture between the client and the therapist.

D. Having too many goals can interfere with the spontaneity and excitement of counseling.

5. My responsibility as a therapist should be primarily:
   A. Assisting clients in creating a new life story.
   B. Helping them make their unconscious become conscious.
   C. Providing brief therapy to deal with the symptom at hand and move forward.
   D. Teaching them responsible, realistic, and appropriate behavior.

6. My main focus as the counselor should be on:
   A. What the client is thinking.
   B. What the client is feeling.
   C. What the client's behavior is.
   D. It depends upon what stage are therapy sessions are in.
   E. What my hourly rate is.

7. Basically I feel that counseling is a process of:
   A. Reeducation.
   B. Re-parenting.
   C. Teaching how to integrate feelings with behaviors.
   D. Learning how to cope with life.
   E. A job.

8. Effective counseling and therapy should focus on:
   A. The client's past experiences.
   B. The client's childhood.
   C. The client's relationship with their mother.
   D. The present only.
   E. The future.

9. In dealing with a multicultural clientele, it is first important to:
   A. Come to terms with my own culture.
   B. Get fieldwork experience in multicultural settings.
   C. Get specialized coursework on various cultures.
   D. Date somebody from another culture.

10. Gaining specific knowledge about other cultures is:

A. Essential for effective counseling.
B. Can be dangerous because of the tendency to stereotype and profile.
C. Impossible because there were too many cultures to know about all.
D. Useful.

PART TWO

1. The client's early childhood experiences are:
   A. Much overblown by Freud and therefore less time should be spent with talking about them. Deal with TODAY.
   B. The childhood experiences influence 100% of what we are today.
   C. Always need to be explored in therapy.
   D. Can influence and explain much of a person's adult behavior.

2. I think the most important purpose of the therapist is:
   A. To be present for and with the client on their journey.
   B. To interpret the meaning of the client's behavior and symptoms.
   C. To provide healthy parenting for the client.
   D. To make the client feel like they have a reason to live.

3. I think that all counselors should:
   A. Take their cues from the client.
   B. Be very interactive and directive.
   C. Listen, and remain quiet, something their parents probably didn't do.
   D. Allow the clients to safely explore their feelings thoughts and anxieties.

4. I feel that for those who are going to become therapists, undergoing therapy:
   A. Should be required for licensing.
   B. Is not important for your clients, and would just serve yourself.
   C. Would indicate that you have problems, so why are you going to

be a therapist?
    D. Would only be necessary if you are suffering from severe personal issues that might get in the way of listening to your clients.

5. By the fact that a client seeks out a therapist, the therapist is given a power by the clients:
    A. This can be used by the therapist to urge direction with the client and their needs.
    B. Can be scary.
    C. Can be the only and vital force that the therapist needs to make changes in the client.
    D. Can certainly reinforce the therapist's ego.

6. To help a client it is better if the therapist:
    A. Has had similar problems.
    B. Has worked out a similar problem and has resolved conflicts.
    C. Must like the client.
    D. Comes from a similar financial, cultural, and religious background.

7. For effective therapy:
    A. The therapist should take the role of friend.
    B. The therapist should take the role of a parent.
    C. Personal warmth is not important.
    D. The therapist must take the role of an expert.

8. A counselor should learn a theory because:
    A. They should select one theory and work with in that framework.
    B. It will give them procedures for an emotional cure.
    C. The more theories that a counselor knows the better chance they find have of finding the one that works for the client.
    D. In time, they should integrate all the theories they know and apply the appropriate techniques as needed for the clients.

9. To be an effective therapist:
    A. The therapist should have a repertoire of counseling concepts.
    B. The therapist needs to know the laws.
    C. The therapist needs to hone their skills in one theory.
    D. The therapist is needs to be open, honest, and with their clients,

theory is not important.

10. Therapists should:
    A. Know themselves.
    B. Have their own lives in order.
    C. Have general goals in mind for all clients before you see them.
    D. Keep your own values outside of therapy.

PART THREE

Comment on the following:

1. Is it imperative that clients and therapists need to have similar values in order to succeed?

2. Should therapy always include positive social and political change if any personal change is to happen?

3. It is appropriate for the therapist to discuss their personal conflicts with the clients, and share how they resolve their own issues?

4. To effectively work with a client, does the therapist have some understanding of the client's culture or be of the same culture?

5. Is one of the most important things for therapist to model the behavior that you are expecting out of your client?

6. Is the kind of person the therapist is, more important than their theoretical orientation?

7. Is it important for the therapist to realize that the client is the real expert in their own lives?

8. Confrontation can interfere with therapy, and make for discomfort in the client, therefore is it generally unwise to ever use confrontation in therapy?

9. The therapist own needs are not important in effective therapy, and need to be left aside.

10. "Silence is golden." Therefore, should the therapist respect that and keep as silent as possible?

PART FOUR

Comment on the following:

1. Because silence indicates boredom on the part of the client, should the therapist do everything they can to avoid silent moments?

2. What is meant by a dual relationship with a client?

3. How do you feel about shopping at a client's store, being at their restaurant, or using their professional services?

4. A therapist is in a role of strength, therefore you must avoid mistakes or lose respect from the client?

5. Can therapy either be positive or negative on the client? How?

6. Is it good or okay, to be flexible in the therapy session even if you had planned on focusing on an issue, or the client had planned on focusing on an issue?

7. Does a therapist have to remain objective, and distant from the client, and not get involved in any way into their personal stuff?

8. As a therapist, I am not a judge. Do I have the right to judge their decisions in business, in their relationships, or in the way they handle their families or children?

9. If I experience intense feelings towards my client (anger, annoyance, boredom, or sexual attraction), will I no longer be effective and should terminate further sessions?

10. Is touching a client inappropriate, under any circumstances?

PART FIVE

1. The outcome of therapy, is based primarily on:
    A. The skills and techniques that the counselor.
    B. The theoretical orientation of the counselor.
    C. The kind of person the counselor is - warmth, charisma, honest?
    D. The willingness of the client to change.

2. Which of the following of the most important personal characteristics of a therapist?
    A. Sense of humor.

B. Theoretical orientation.
C. Being present and THERE for the client.
D. Having resolved their own personal problems.

3. If you go into therapy prior to becoming a therapist, what issues would you consider most pertinent to address from your own life?
A. Unfinished situations from my past, especially looking at the relationship with my parents.
B. My fear of getting too close to my clients, and taking on their issues.
C. My anxieties of failure and/or causing harm with my clients.
D. General anxiety of being a counselor with a person's life in my hands.

4. What is causing you the greatest anxiety when you think about being a counselor?
A. Afraid I might not have the knowledge or skills to be effective.
B. Making mistakes that could hurt the client.
C. Dealing with a suicidal client, and having them commit suicide.
D. Burnout, as I find out this is not the career for me.

5. How would you determine the effectiveness or appropriateness of self-disclosure?
A. Doing what feels comfortable at the time.
B. Observing and respecting, that self-disclosure is never appropriate.
C. Watching the client's response as I slowly self disclose.
D. By monitoring my own motivation for gauging and self-disclosure.

6. When do you think it might be important to disclose yourself to clients?
A. When they asked me questions about themselves, but those issues have also impacted me in my past.
B. When I want to influence the clients to grow.
C. When I feel that sharing, shows caring.
D. When I have persistent reactions to their issues.

7. Silences in a therapy session would:
A. Feel threatening to me, I would think I've done something wrong.
B. I would ask questions of the client to get them moving again.

C. I would discuss with the client my discomfort about their silence.

D. I would play psychoanalyst, and sit quietly and wait for the client to take initiative.

8. What is the role of giving advice in therapy?

9. What is the role of humor in therapy?

10. If you tend to be anal retentive and somewhat obsessive yourself, will this be a boon to your therapy or a hindrance?

PART SIX

1. Is sarcasm okay in therapy and play a role? And if so, when?

2. Is it appropriate, or effective, to have a small pet in the office? And if so, why?

3. How would you prevent burnout?

4. How do you expect that you would go about developing your own counseling style?

5. As a counselor, I expect that my values will affect my counseling process in what following ways-

6. I know the law requires counselors to take law and ethics classes continually, but I feel if you're not ethical, you shouldn't be in this business because:

7. One of the motivations for being in the therapy business is a desire to nurture others, comment on how that motivation impacts or helps?

8. I was always told I was a good listener; therefore it is now my desire to be able to give advice to those who have problems. Comment.

9. A therapist's personal values should be kept out of the therapy session at all times. Comment.

10. If a client evidenced strong feelings of attraction or dislike for me I would feel that I have to:
    A. Help the client work through those feelings and understand them.
    B. Feel complemented and enjoy those feelings if they are positive.
    C. Refer my client to another therapist.
    D. Change the thrust of the sessions and into something that is less emotionally involved.

PART SEVEN

1. I saw a T-shirt one time that said "Comfort the disturbed, disturb the comfortable." Comment on the quote, and how it might apply to counseling and therapy.

2. Since the purpose of counseling is not to teach values to the clients, or to teach them your values, but it is to teach clients how to discover their own values. How would you do that?

3. Why do you think it is not good to reveal your own values to clients lest you bias the direction your clients are likely to take in working with you?

4. To what degree do you think it is possible for you to disagree with the clients values, and yet still accept him or her as a person in therapy? And provide them good counseling?

5. Can you think of the situation when it might be justified for you to impose your values on the clients?

6. How would you handle it if you discovered that there is a sharp value conflict between you and your client, such as working with a perpetrator of sex crimes or child abuse?

7. How would you handle a client who comes in to discuss an extramarital affair, and they really are looking for your approval of it?

8. How would you handle the client above if you happen to know his wife, or kids, or any of his family members? What if he was attending your church congregation?

9. How would you handle an adolescent girl who discusses the fact that sex is not so bad because she can always have an abortion?

10. How would you handle a client who you perceive is taking advantage of others in their business?

_____

PART EIGHT

1. How would you handle a client who comes in with an issue over a friend who belongs to the same church denomination that you do, and she is going on about how bad that church is, ridiculing their belief system, and therefore your's as well?

2. How about the client who knows everybody else is "stupid" and if they just live by his values and understood his way, things would be fine?

3. How about the client who is a 14-year-old high school student, and feels she may be a lesbian because of an attraction she has toward one of her female teachers?

4. You have a 35-year-old, single male client who has just lost his job, he's single, and discusses the fact that he has a 9 mm gun in his car that he is struggling with NOT using it. What do you say?

5. You have a 33-year-old female client, who is doing a significant amount of drugs, and discloses to you that for the first half of her life her father who is a well-known person in your neighborhood has been sexually abusing her. What do you say? How do you handle it?

6. How do you think your own values, and your own spiritual beliefs, will support you through your career as a counselor?

7. How comfortable do you feel you would be when a 10-year-old boy who you are seeing for acting out problems, tells you that the only real problem is that mom caught him masturbating?

8. What would you tell the teenager who you are seeing for depression,

when they ask you what you think they should do, now that mom and dad are divorcing, and they will be asked who they want to live with?

9. Do you think it would be appropriate to ask a client who is of either a different culture or different religion than your's, to explain some of their beliefs and cultural norms?

10. With what issues would you feel more comfortable in referring your client to another counselor? When and how would you do that?

PART NINE

1. What do you consider your personal strengths that will make you a better counselor?

2. As a counselor, are there any personal limitations you feel you have that you need to work on before becoming a counselor?

3. What are your specific anxieties about working as a counselor?

4. How would you handle a client who rejects you or rejects a technique or suggestion? For instance, if you suggest the client use "the empty chair technique" to talk with their dead mother, and they tell you that your idea is just "stupid."

5. How will you know when it is time to terminate a client session.? Is there a specific way to know?

6. How will you handle the client who says they feel like they are well and everything is fine so they want to terminate, and you know there are still major issues to deal with?

7. Do you know what a dual relationship is? How do you define it?

8. What is the role of confidentiality in therapy? Do you discuss this with the client?

9. Are there appropriate times to break confidentiality? What is the Tarasoff rule? Explain it.

10. What is your definition of an ethical therapist?

PART TEN

Comment on the following.

1. "The key to understanding human behavior lies in understanding the unconscious."

2. "Often in counseling, the transference issue where the therapist becomes a healthy parent, can be very productive."

3. "All negative behaviors can be modified, and/or extinguished, once the client understands the thought process instigating the behaviors."

4. "No effective therapy can happen without being deep into the childhood."

16

5. "Often there are no good reasons to stir up old memories or repressed memories if they are just going to cause your client sadness."

6. How would you effect producing a therapy environment of warm detachment?

7. Prior to taking this class or other psych classes, were there any psychotherapy theories or modes that you had heard of? What were they?

8. How important do you think your client's position in the family of origin will impact their therapy or has impacted their lives?

9. When will you know a client has internalized the insight they might have come to in your sessions? For instance, new members of AA often will intellectualize, and discuss how wonderful iced tea is, but they have not internalized yet to a comfortableness about sobriety, and the truth is they would still prefer a beer. Are they only giving you "lip-service".

10. How will you know if you are a successful therapist?

Transference

What is Transference?

During transference, people turn into a "biological time machine". A nerve is struck when someone says or does something that reminds you of your past. This creates an "emotional time warp" that transfers your emotional past and your psychological needs into the present. In less poetic terms, a transference reaction means that you are reacting to someone in terms of what you need to see in them, or that you are afraid of what you will see eventually even though you know very little about the person. This all happens without you knowing why you feel and react the way you do. You are ascribing emotions, thoughts, feelings to a person based on your past. Clients will often transfer "parenting" feelings to you that were missing at home, or were present at home and not resolved.

What Is Projection?

Some people refer to transference as a "projection." In this case you are projecting your own feelings, emotions or motivations into another person without realizing your reaction is really more about you than it is about the other person. In a life filled with transference, your job may be "the family reunion you are avoiding and you are forced to go to each day." In other cases of projection, your girlfriend may remind you of all the irritating things your mother did when you were growing up. Love at first sight is usually a projection – especially if it ends in disaster and you could have seen it coming.

Extreme Transference

In an extreme form of transference, you may conclude that someone is an awful or evil person when in fact that person's favorite food and television show reminds you of an emotionally abusive mother and a sexually abusive brother you have been trying to forget since childhood. That's an example of **negative** transference. A warm, supportive and kind person could remind you of what you are missing and wanting in their life. You might then idealize that person and begin to see him or her as wonderful beyond belief. The idea is that you will react to your therapist based on your experience with another person. It is usually apparent that the patient has an unresolved conflict with. In extreme cases a patient will become overly attached to their therapist or they will enter into and create conflicts without realizing how.

Transference Melt-Downs

Extreme forms of transference can turn into a full-blown obsession if it is not dealt with. Transference "meltdowns" can result in accidents, dangerous choices, nightmares, fantasies, stalking someone, psychotic reactions and sometimes violence. While it does not happen frequently in therapy, it can happen in the patient's personal life.

How Can You Tell?

How do you know you are having a "transference reaction"? It's not always easy, but you probably are if you know very little about a client (or anyone) and you are having a powerful reaction that is not justifiable to a reasonable person. It can be difficult if the patient can rationalize their reactions. Having a strong sexual attraction to your therapist is almost always a transference reaction, unless of course your therapist is actually hitting on you – which they are not supposed to do on purpose.

Intentionally seducing a vulnerable patient is sick and wrong! In fact that applies to any health-related profession or any employer-employee relationship. Becoming angry at your therapist as if they were a parent is a good sign that there is a transference reaction. Termination of treatment pre-maturely is another sign of transference - unless the therapist is just doing a bad job.

Counter-Transference

Therapists and other health care professionals can also have transference reactions while treating a patient. It's a two way street. Counter-transference is basically a therapist's "emotional time warp" around their patient's transference. In other words, counter-transference is a therapist's counter-reaction. That's why some therapists think they are falling in love with their patients. That's also why older guys become obsessed with younger female employees they barely know.

Unseen Dangers

Transference can sometimes produce a powerful love or a destructive hatred based on a complete illusion. There can be a loud and painful thud when people act on their transference reactions and the bubble finally bursts. In addition to being embarrassed, it can also backfire. Sometimes people will end up stalking, assaulting or killing someone.

Should I or Shouldn't I Risk Transference

Transference is really difficult to recognize, deal with and understand, but it is incredibly interesting. Working with transference, or creating transference in therapy can make a therapist look mystical and brilliant. Cult therapies are based in part on generating positive transference to control and manipulate people. Some counselors and therapists love the power and think they can handle it. A therapist must face transference issues and encourage patients to deal with them as much as possible. In some cases a patient is not able to deal with transference issues and will terminate therapy. While it is regrettable and potentially a lost opportunity, it must be supported.

> When childhood dies,
> its corpses are called adults and they enter society,
> one of the politer names of hell.
> That is why we dread children, even if we love them.
> They show us the state of our decay.
> - Brian Aldiss

What Freud says about transference and counter-transference during psychotherapy

In a therapy context, **transference** refers to redirection of a client's feelings from a significant person to a therapist. Transference is often manifested as an erotic attraction towards a therapist, but can be seen in many other forms such as rage, hatred, mistrust, parentification, extreme dependence, or even placing the therapist in a god-like or guru status. When Freud initially encountered transference in his therapy with clients, he felt it was an obstacle to treatment success. But what he learned was that the analysis of the transference was actually the work that needed to be done. The focus in psychodynamic psychotherapy is, in large part, the therapist and client recognizing the transference relationship and exploring what the meaning of the relationship is. Because the transference between patient and therapist happens on an unconscious level, psychodynamic therapists who are largely concerned with a patient's unconscious material use the transference to reveal unresolved conflicts patients have with figures from their childhoods.

Ego, Id, Super-Ego

The structure of the personality in psychoanalytic theory is threefold. Freud divided it into the Id, the Ego, and the Superego. Only the ego was visible or on the surface, while the Id and the superego remain below, but each have their own effects on the personality, nonetheless.

The Id represents biological forces. It is also a constant in the personality as it is always present. The Id is governed by the "pleasure principle", or the notion of hedonism (the seeking of pleasure). Early in the development of his theory Freud saw sexual energy only, or the libido, or the life instinct, as the only source of energy for the Id. It was this notion that gave rise to the popular conception that psychoanalysis was all about sex, sex, sex. After the carnage of World War I, however, Freud felt it necessary to add another instinct, or source of energy, to the Id. So, he proposed Thanatos, the death instinct. Thanatos accounts for the instinctual violent urges of humankind. Obviously, the rest of the personality would have to somehow deal with these two instincts. Notice how Hollywood has capitalized on the Id. Box office success is highly correlated with movies that stress either sex, violence, or both.

The ego is the surface of the personality, the part you show the world. The ego is governed by the "reality principle," or a pragmatic approach to the world. For example, a child may want to snitch a cookie from the kitchen, but will not if a parent is present. Id desires are still present, but the ego realizes the consequences of brazen cookie theft. The ego develops with experience, and accounts for developmental differences in behavior. For example, parents expect 3-month infants to cry until fed, but they also expect 3-year-olds to stop crying when told they will be fed.

The superego consists of two parts, the conscience and the ego-ideal. The conscience is the familiar metaphor of angel and devil on each shoulder. The conscience decides what course of action one should take. The ego-ideal is an idealized view of one's self. Comparisons are made between the ego-ideal and one's actual behavior. Both parts of the super-ego develop with experience with others, or via social interactions. According to Freud, a strong super-ego serves to inhibit the biological instincts of the Id, while a weak super-ego gives in to the Id's urgings. Further, the levels of guilt in the two cases above will be high and low, respectively.

The tripartite structure above was thought to be dynamic, changing with age and experience. Also, aspects of adult behavior such as smoking, neatness, and need for sexual behavior were linked to the various stages by fixation. To Freud, fixation is a measure of the effort required to travel through any particular stage, and great efforts in childhood were reflected in adult behavior. Fixation can also be interpreted as the learning of patterns or habits. Part of the criticism of psychoanalysis was that fixation could be interpreted in diametrically opposite fashion. For example, fixation in the anal stage could lead to excessive neatness or sloppiness. As noted earlier, Neil Simon's play, "The Odd Couple", is a celebration of anal fixation, with Oscar and Felix representing the two opposite ends of the fixation continuum (Oscar-sloppy, Felix-neat).

What Is The Difference Between Counseling and Psychotherapy? Or Psychiatry? Or Life Coaching?

There are many myths about what counseling and psychotherapy entail. Most of them are rooted in outdated ideas about psychology and psychotherapy, or what folks have seen on TV and in the movies - usually images of old men in beards with their clients on couches or patients in locked up asylums where they scream and yell a lot. People often dismiss counseling as:
- Something for "crazy people"?
- Professional help for people only who have really major problems
- An activity for people who are way too preoccupied with themselves
- A crutch for people who are just too weak to handle life
- Where you go and get analyzed by somebody
  and then hope something changes for the better

Counseling/psychotherapy is not just a place that people go to find out if they're "crazy", but rather to get support because sometimes the world around them can seem pretty "crazy". Counseling is not something that attends only to challenges regarded as "major problems" and dismisses things some may regard as "less important problems" but rather attends to the issues that clients bring in whenever they feel the distress is getting in the way of living life with satisfaction. Counseling strives to help show those who come to counseling that they possess the strength and abilities to manage their life challenges. Counseling, more than psychotherapy, is not an activity where the shrink analyzes the client but rather an activity where counselor and client work as a team to make positive changes in the client's approach to life. Counseling and therapy is not a crutch for weak people, but can be a vehicle for stronger people who decide to face their challenges directly rather than continue in the more frightened and escape-oriented ways that others use to deal with difficulties.

Counseling/therapy is a unique relationship in which the Counselor's job is to hold up a mirror for the client to see himself or herself in. We all have experiences in which we can't see things about ourselves without a mirror. Often we have deep-seated stuff that is in a hard to see place - our minds. The deaf client is easily seen as deaf. We should know how to react, the hearing aids, are visual clues that give their problem away. But the sexually or emotionally abused person can hide their pain, and we don't know. They will often work very, very hard at concealing their issues and pain. In addition to knowing what angles to hold the mirror from, the counselor needs to understand that sometimes it takes a while for clients to see what they need, especially if there are more subtle things needing our recognition.

In teaching the field of psychotherapy, I often suggest that I get two types of clients: One who comes in and knows their problem and we work to resolve it. The second type comes in because others say they have a problem, but they don't see it. And of those two, often the problem is very obvious to the therapist, but hard to get across to the client, or it is very hard to zero in to the 'ah-ha' where the therapist now has a handle on their issue, even if they don't yet!

A good sensitive counselor knows how to hold that mirror in such a way that the client can see himself or herself from a caring, supportive, and sympathetic perspective. In other words, the therapist, often, becomes a surrogate parent, which can lead to the transference and counter-transference issues we will talk about.

So, what is the difference between counseling and psychotherapy? Here are the answers and ideas of students, online results and your professor's. What it points out is there is NO black and white answer and most of Mr. and Mrs. America, have NO clue! They just go to their doctor, whether the person is a Ph.D., M.A., B.A., or a self appointed expert.

Generally, a **counselor** is someone who works with another to assist with problem solving and offers advice on how to work through a problem, generally short-term. Counselors concentrate on the behavioral aspects of the person while looking at a particular problem or situation, with suggestions on how to improve the situation. Counselors do not necessarily have to have specialized training. Counselors are available to help people with all kinds of needs: financial planning, spiritual, marriage and family, etc.

If someone is experiencing emotional distress, feeling depressed, or going through a crisis; they may be feeling confused or wish to develop a greater degree of self-understanding. It may be just that they need someone to talk to who is outside their family and circle of friends, who has no preconceived ideas about them so the counselor can give fresh insights into how they feel and respond to things. This can often give them the support, understanding and trust, that they may not have been able to get from their family and friends.

Psychotherapists try to gain insight into physical and emotional problems by looking at the client's way of thought processing and less at attacking a particular problem. The psychotherapist has a much broader view of the whole person's mental health and generally offers longer-term care than a counselor. Generally, more training is required for a psychotherapist than for a counselor and it is usually someone trained specifically in psychotherapy, e.g., psychiatrist, MFT, clinical psychologist. Often the difference is a psychotherapist can provide counseling but generally a counselor does not have the training to provide psychotherapy.

Psychotherapy generally is a talking treatment that aims to help you to find ways of coping with problems you may be experiencing. The therapist's "pills" are words versus the psychiatrist's pills being PILLS! Medication, and often, over medication can be the bane of therapy. The overall aim of psychotherapy is to help you to understand why you feel the way you do, and what lies behind your responses to other people and to things that happen to you. Many people find that this understanding helps them to deal more successfully with problems and stress. Psychotherapy provides an opportunity for you to work towards living in a more satisfying and resourceful way by developing your understanding of yourself and the way you respond to others.

The psychotherapeutic process generally goes deeper than counseling as you may be encouraged to look closely at your past, particularly your childhood, and your relationships with significant people in your life.

Psychotherapy involves talking to someone who is trained to listen. Psychotherapy can take a number of forms, but is generally longer-term than other talking treatments such as counseling or cognitive behavior therapy. The expected time-scale for undergoing psychotherapy should be seen in terms of years rather than weeks or months. Psychotherapy can vary according to which school of thought the therapist adheres to, but the basic therapeutic principles of providing a safe environment where you can talk about what is troubling you and be listened to in an empathic manner remain the same.

A **psychiatrist** is a medical doctor who has received graduate training in psychology. They may also have either a Ph.D. or a Psy.D. in clinical or counseling psychology. Schooling normally involves five to eight years of graduate studies in the specialized field. They receive specific training in treatment, assessment, diagnosis, and prevention of mental illnesses as well as in pharmacology. Psychiatrists also often do research. Since psychiatrists have an M.D., they can prescribe medication. Psychiatry is the field of medicine which deals with the diagnosis, treatment and prevention of mental, emotional and behavioral disorders. It integrates biological, sociological and psychological aspects of mental health to provide holistic medical care for a wide range of symptoms.

There are many fields in psychiatry including general adult, child and adolescent, eating disorders, old age, substance dependence, forensic, and neuropsychiatry.

A **Life Coach** can be anyone. There are many ads on the internet for schools to teach life coaching, and there are no restrictions or requirements for a person to call himself a life coach. Ordinary people with no particular background in psychology or psychiatry are on the internet advertising their services to make you a better someone. Life coaches can help people reach goals to improve their current behavior, usually specializing in a particular area. Some use psychology and counseling concepts. Generally, they are not therapists and should not be making psychological evaluation. Life coaches inspire and stir up a group, usually focusing on a particular topic like career or financial growth such as Tony Robbins. Goal setting is a large part of a life coach's inspiration to their clients. They can be very motivational, but just because they are recognized as good speakers, does not necessarily mean that they are trained in professional counseling.

I suggest you think of the Pop-Warner football coach who deals with younger kids to get the coach slant. When he works with kids, he is working on their strengths and attempts to make them better. I.e., they are athletic, and he wants them to be better athletes. When he works with them, he tries to get them to enhance their abilities and talents on the football field. If Johnny gets sacked in a game, and is whimpering and crying, he does not ask him how he is doing. He does not care if there are problems at home that kept him from playing well. He doesn't care if Grandma is having cancer surgery, what he does is say, "Shake it off and get out there and play. Hit 'em hard and you'll be fine." The charismatic preacher is also a 'life coach' saying things like, "Jesus loves you, and is behind you. You can do ANYTHING with God's support. ANYTHING. ANYTHING is possible if you just believe." Unfortunately some also suggest more financial support of the church will help too. BUT, the point is, the preacher is not concerned about your childhood at that point, nor your physical deformities, etc, but just that YOU can do it, and with God's support, you will believe in yourself and you WILL do it.

Partly that works, and partly it doesn't. Adrenalin pumping gets a lot more done than we would ever expect. The extra bucks to the night-time TV preachers, probably doesn't!

What is "Mental Illness" that these folks work with?

One in five people suffer from emotional problems sufficiently distressing to justify seeking professional help. Their symptoms can range from relatively mild feelings of depression and anxiety to severe distress and dysfunction, which threatens life itself. Unfortunately, many people with mental illnesses and emotional problems fail to seek the professional help that they need. Scientific, medical and social research is enabling a better understanding of the nature and cause of psychiatric illnesses and symptoms, and improved ways of diagnosing and treating them are constantly being developed.

Mental illness is any disease or condition affecting the brain that negatively influences the way a person thinks, feels, behaves and/or relates to others and to his or her surroundings. Although the symptoms of mental illness can range from mild to severe and are different depending on the type of mental illness, a person with an untreated mental illness often is unable to cope with life's daily routines and demands.

What Causes Mental Illness?

Although the exact cause of most mental illnesses is not known, it is becoming clear through research that many of these conditions are caused by a combination of genetic, biological, psychological and environmental factors. One thing is for sure - mental illness is not the result of personal weakness or a character defect, and recovery from a mental illness is not simply a matter of will and self-discipline.

Heredity (genetics):

Many mental illnesses run in families, suggesting that the illnesses may be passed on from parents to children through genes. Genes contain instructions for the function of each cell in the body and are responsible for how we look, act, think, etc. But, just because your mother or father may have a mental illness doesn't mean you will have one. Hereditary just means that you are more likely to get the condition than if you didn't have an affected family member. Experts believe that many mental conditions are linked to problems in multiple genes - not just one, as with many diseases, which is why a person inherits a susceptibility to a mental disorder, but doesn't always develop the condition. The disorder itself occurs from the interaction of these genes and other factors - such as psychological trauma and environmental stressors - which can influence, or trigger, the illness in a person who has inherited a susceptibility to it.

Biology:

Some mental illnesses have been linked to an abnormal balance of special chemicals in the brain called neurotransmitters. Neurotransmitters help nerve cells in the brain communicate with each other. If these chemicals are out of balance or are not working properly, messages may not make it through the brain correctly, leading to symptoms of mental illness. In addition, defects in or injury to certain areas of the brain also have been linked to some mental conditions.

Psychological trauma:
Some mental illnesses may be triggered by psychological trauma suffered as a child, such as severe emotional, physical or sexual abuse; a significant early loss, such as the loss of a parent; and neglect.

Environmental stressors:
Certain stressors - such as a death or divorce, a dysfunctional family life, changing jobs or schools and substance abuse - can trigger a disorder in a person who may be at risk for developing a mental illness.

How Common Is Mental Illness?
Unfortunately, most mental illnesses are caused by a combination of factors and cannot be prevented. Mental illnesses are very common. In fact, they are more common than cancer, diabetes or heart disease. According to the U.S. Surgeon General, an estimated 23% of American adults (those ages 18 and older), about 44 million people, and about 20% of American children suffer from a mental disorder during a given year. Further, about 5 million Americans adults, and more than 5 million children and adolescents suffer from a serious mental condition (one that significantly interferes with functioning).

Major depression, bipolar disorder and schizophrenia are among the U.S.'s top 10 leading causes of disability.

Mental illness does not discriminate. It can affect people of any age, income or education level, or cultural background. Although mental illness affects both males and females, certain conditions—such as eating disorders - tend to occur more often in females, and other disorders - such as attention-deficit/hyperactivity disorder (ADHD) - more commonly occur in children.

How Is Mental Illness Treated?
A mental illness, like many chronic illnesses, requires ongoing treatment. Fortunately, much progress has been made in the last two decades in treating mental illnesses.

As a result, many mental conditions can be effectively treated with one or a combination of the following therapies:

Medication
Psychotherapy
Group therapy
Day treatment or partial hospital treatment
Specific therapies, such as CBT and behavior modification

Other treatments available include:
Alternative therapies, such as water therapy, massage and
biofeedback
Creative therapies, such as art therapy, music therapy or play therapy
Hypnotherapy
Electroconvulsive therapy (ECT)

What Is the Outlook for People with Mental Illness?

When diagnosed early and treated properly, many people fully recover from their mental disorder or are able to successfully control their symptoms. Although some people become disabled because of a chronic or severe mental illness, many others are able to live full and productive lives. In fact, as many as 8 in 10 people suffering from a mental illness can effectively return to their normal activities if they receive appropriate treatment

In the past, the subject of mental illness was surrounded with mystery and fear. Today, we have made tremendous progress in our understanding and, especially in our ability to offer effective treatments. However, questions about mental illness often go unanswered and stand in the way of people receiving help.

How Common Is Mental Illness and What Are the Impacts on Society?

Mental illness is common, and the milder conditions are very common. One fifth of Americans suffer from a diagnosable mental disorder during any given year. One fifth of school-age children are also affected by these conditions. Severe and persistent mental illness is less common, but still afflicts three percent of the population.

The vast majority of individuals with mental disorders continue to function in their daily lives, although with varying impairments. Overall medical care costs are driven up enormously by costs associated with unrecognized psychiatric syndromes.

Are People Suffering from Mental Illnesses Violent?

There is a misconception that people with mental illnesses are violent, which contributes to the stigma of mental illness. The vast majority of people with mental illness are not violent, and the majority of violent acts are conducted by persons who are not mentally ill. They are more likely to be victims of violence than perpetrators, and more likely to hurt themselves than hurt other people.

Do Psychiatrists(M.D.'s) Do More than Just Write Prescriptions for their Patients?

Psychiatric treatment involves a full mental and physical health evaluation and an individualized treatment plan, which may include psychotherapy (talk therapy), medication, or other modalities. Psychiatrists help patients understand illnesses and understand what they can do to resolve life problems that contribute to illnesses. This may involve issues on the job, in school, or within the family and community.

Psychiatrists see the necessity of working within a tailored approach for the treatment of their patients. Educational, medical, spiritual, and interpersonal as well as basic issues such as adequate housing and nutrition are considered. Sometimes the misuse of drugs or alcohol is present and will require treatment.

Today's model of psychiatric care recognizes the importance of families as part of the treatment team. Interventions which help families struggling with child abuse and neglect, domestic and community violence, substance abuse, or school failure increasingly integrate psychiatric consultation into their programs. Any or all of these interventions may be used in tailoring a treatment plan for patients.

SECTION II
THEORIES OVERVIEW

"Conflict. Conflict? Human relationships are filled with conflict. Because of this, the whole planet Earth is filled with conflict. Not that that's a bad thing - because it's through conflict that we learn about ourselves. Here on our perfect planet, we have no emotion or conflicts so we've never had to look inward at ourselves. And while that's helped us become a technological intellectual force in the universe, you know I really think - it's a dead end! On our planet, all emotions have been bred out of this race and each succeeding generation has become more ambitious and driven than the previous one."

Cognitive Behavior Therapy

Cognitive behavior therapy is the most popular therapy style now, and REQUIRED by insurance programs. CBT has become the preferred treatment for conditions such as these when the person has insurance, and in most therapy offices.

Depression and mood swings
Shyness and social anxiety
Panic attacks and phobias
Obsessions and compulsions (OCD and related conditions)
Chronic anxiety or worry
Post-traumatic stress symptoms (PTSD and related conditions)
Eating disorders (anorexia and bulimia) and obesity
Insomnia and other sleep problems
Difficulty establishing or staying in relationships
Problems with marriage or other relationships you're already in
Job, career or school difficulties
Feeling "stressed out"
Insufficient self-esteem accepting or respecting yourself)
Inadequate coping skills, or ill-chosen methods of coping
Passivity, procrastination and "passive aggression"
Substance abuse, co-dependency and "enabling"
Trouble keeping feelings such as anger, sadness, fear, guilt, shame, eagerness, excitement, etc., within bounds
Over-inhibition of feelings or expression

Just what is CBT and how does it work?

Cognitive behavior therapy combines two kinds of psychotherapy cognitive therapy and behavior therapy:

Behavior therapy helps the client weaken the connections between troublesome situations and their habitual reactions to them such as fear, depression or rage, and self-defeating or self-damaging behavior. It also teaches the client how to calm their mind and body, so the client can feel better, think more clearly, and make better decisions.

Cognitive therapy teaches the client how certain thinking patterns are causing their symptoms - by giving the client a distorted picture of what's going on in their life, and making the client feel anxious, depressed or angry for no good reason, or provoking the client into ill-chosen actions. When combined into CBT, behavior therapy and cognitive therapy provide the client with very powerful tools for stopping their symptoms and getting their life on a more satisfying track.

The preferred term, Cognitive Behavior Therapy, gives the behavioral components of CBT more emphasis. This is in line with the history of CBT, as well as being better supported by outcome research.

CBT is active therapy

In CBT, the therapist takes an active part in solving the client problems. He or she doesn't settle for just nodding wisely while **the client** carries the whole burden of finding the answers the client came to therapy for as in psychoanalytic work.

CBT usually provides a diagnostic work-up at the beginning of treatment to make sure their needs and problems have been pinpointed as well as possible. This crucial step, which is often skimped or omitted altogether in traditional kinds of therapy, results in an explicit, understandable, and flexible treatment plan that accurately reflects their own individual needs.

In many ways CBT resembles education, coaching or tutoring. Under expert guidance, a CBT client will share in setting treatment goals and in deciding which techniques work best for them personally.

Structured and focused

CBT provides clear structure and focus to treatment. Unlike therapies that easily drift off into interesting but unproductive side trips, CBT sticks to the point and changes course only when there are sound reasons for doing so.

A CBT client will often take on "homework" projects to speed their progress. These assignments extend and multiply the results of the work done in the therapist's office. Often they receive take-home readings and other materials tailored to their needs to help.

What else is different about CBT?

Most people coming for therapy need to change something in their lives whether it's the way they feel, the way they act, or how other people treat them. CBT focuses on finding out just what needs to be changed and what doesn't and then works for those targeted changes.

Some exploration of people's life histories is necessary and desirable if their current problems are closely tied to "unfinished emotional business" from the past, or if they grow out of a repeating pattern of difficulty. Nevertheless, 100 years of psychotherapy has made this clear.

Past vs. Present vs. Future

Focusing on the past (and on dreams) can at times help **explain** a person's difficulties. But these activities all too often do little to actually overcome them. Instead, in CBT the aim is rapid improvement in feelings and moods, and early changes in any self-defeating behavior the client may be caught up in. CBT is present-centered and forward-looking vs. traditional therapies.

The Levers of Change

The two most powerful levers of constructive change (apart from medication in some cases) in CBT are:

Altering ways of thinking a person's thoughts, beliefs, ideas, attitudes, assumptions, mental imagery, and ways of directing his or her attention for the better. This is the **cognitive** aspect of CBT.

Helping a person greet the challenges and opportunities in his or her life with a clear and calm mind and then taking actions that are likely to have desirable results. This is the **behavioral** aspect of CBT.

CBT therapists feel they focuses on exactly what they feel traditional therapies don't.

To wrap up, Cognitive behavioral therapy (or cognitive behavioral therapies or CBT) is a psychotherapeutic approach that aims to solve problems concerning dysfunctional emotions, behaviors and cognitions through a goal-oriented, systematic procedure. The title is used in diverse ways to designate behavior therapy, cognitive therapy, and to refer to therapy based upon a combination of basic behavioral and cognitive research.

There is research that CBT is effective for the treatment of a variety of problems, including mood, anxiety, personality, eating, substance abuse, and psychotic disorders. CBT is used in individual therapy as well as group settings, and the techniques are often adapted for self-help applications. Some clinicians and researchers are more cognitive oriented (e.g. cognitive restructuring), while others are more behaviorally oriented (in-vivo exposure therapy). Other interventions combine both with imaginal exposure therapy.

CBT was developed through a merging of behavior therapy with cognitive therapy. These two traditions found common ground in focusing on the "here and now" and on alleviating symptoms. The health-care field has favored CBT over other approaches such as psychodynamic treatments of recent.

The roots of CBT can be traced to the development of behavior therapy in the early 20th century, the development of cognitive therapy in the 1960s, and the subsequent merging. Behavior therapeutical approaches appeared as early as 1924, with Mary Cover Jones' work on the unlearning of fears in children. In 1937 Abraham Low developed cognitive training techniques for patient aftercare following psychiatric hospitalization. Low designed his techniques for use in his organization, Recovery International, which supports people recovering from mental illness. Although Recovery International was originally led by Low, he later adapted the techniques for use in lay-run self-help groups operating under the same name.

During the period 1950 to 1970, CBT became widely utilized, inspired by the behaviorist learning theory of Ivan Pavlov, John B. Watson and Clark L. Hull. In Britain, this work was mostly focused on the neurotic disorders through the work of Joseph Wolpe, who applied the findings of animal experiments to his method of systematic desensitization, the precursor to today's fear reduction techniques. British psychologist Hans Eysenck, inspired by the writings of Karl Popper, criticized psychoanalysis in arguing that "if you get rid of the symptoms, you get rid of the neurosis", and presented behavior therapy as a constructive alternative.

In the United States, psychologists were applying the radical behaviorism of B. F. Skinner to clinical use. Much of this work was concentrated towards severe, chronic psychiatric disorders, such as psychotic behavior and autism.

Although the early behavioral approaches were successful in many of the neurotic disorders, they had little success in treating depression. Behaviorism was also losing in popularity due to the so-called "cognitive revolution". The therapeutic approaches of Albert Ellis and Aaron T. Beck gained popularity among behavior therapists, despite the earlier behaviorist rejection of "mentalistic" concepts like thoughts and cognitions. Both these systems included behavioral elements and interventions and primarily concentrated on problems in the present. Albert Ellis's system, originated in the early 1950s, was first called Rational Therapy, and can arguably be called one of the first forms of cognitive behavioral therapy. Cognitive therapy rapidly became a favorite intervention technique to study in psychotherapy research in academic settings. In initial studies, it was often contrasted with behavioral treatments to see which was most effective. During the 1980s and 1990s, cognitive and behavioral techniques were merged into cognitive behavioral therapy.

Concurrently with the contributions of Ellis and Beck, starting in the late 1950s and continuing through the 1970s, Arnold A. Lazarus developed what was arguably the first form of broad-spectrum cognitive behavioral therapy. He later broadened the focus of behavioral treatment to incorporate cognitive aspects. When it became clear that optimizing therapy's effectiveness and effecting durable treatment outcomes often required transcending more narrowly focused cognitive and behavioral methods, Arnold Lazarus expanded the scope of CBT to include physical sensations (as distinct from emotional states), visual images (as distinct from language-based thinking), interpersonal relationships, and biological factors.

Samuel Yochelson and Stanton Samenow pioneered the idea that cognitive behavioral approaches can be used successfully with a criminal population.

CBT NEGATIVES

CBT has come under fire from non-CBT therapists who claim that the data does not fully support the extent of attention and funding it receives nor its extension beyond psychotherapy into matters such as reducing unemployment, and that the limitations of the CBT model when used to blanket-address psychological suffering are unrecognized. Psychotherapist and professor Andrew Samuels stated that this constitutes "a coup, a power play by a community that has suddenly found itself on the brink of corralling an enormous amount of money. Science isn't the appropriate perspective from which to look at emotional difficulties. Everyone has been seduced by CBT's apparent low cost/cheapness. The managed care insurance programs love it!"

Presenters at a psychotherapy conference in 2008 criticized the widespread belief that CBT is more effective than other forms of psychotherapy. Their thrust was that as more research focuses on CBT, more studies are published on CBT which in turn reinforces the logical error that CBT is superior and this has a direct negative effect on other forms of therapy, which are well documented but have smaller bodies of research. What is known, is that people who get ANY therapy improve substantially, regardless of the type of therapy they get. When therapies are compared to one another, they usually appear to be equally effective. Excessive spending on CBT research and marketing, and thus discourages other forms of therapy and hurts the public.

At the same conference, more than 80 studies showed that person-centered psychotherapy was shown to be as effective as other forms of psychotherapy, including CBT. In a 2010 article in Psychological Medicine entitled, "Cognitive behavioral therapy for the major psychiatric disorder: does it really work?" The authors found that no trial employing both blinding and psychological placebo has found CBT to be effective in schizophrenia. The authors also found few well-controlled studies of CBT in depression that found the therapy to be effective, but the size of the effect is small, and CBT is also ineffective in preventing relapses in bipolar disorder.

Psychoanalysis

Psychoanalysis (or Freudian psychology) is a body of ideas developed by Austrian physician Sigmund Freud and continued by others. It is primarily devoted to the study of human psychological functioning and behavior, although it can also be applied to societies. Psychoanalysis has three applications:
1.   a method of investigation of the mind and the way one thinks;
2.   a systematized set of theories about human behavior;
3.   a method of treatment of psychological or emotional illness.

Under the broad umbrella of what is psychoanalysis, there are at least

22 theoretical orientations regarding the underlying theory of understanding of human mentation (the process or result of mental activity) and human development. The various approaches in treatment called "psychoanalytic" vary as much as the theories do. The term also refers to a method of studying child development.

Freudian psychoanalysis refers to a specific type of treatment in which the "analysand" (analytic patient) verbalizes thoughts, including free associations, fantasies, and dreams, from which the analyst formulates the unconscious conflicts causing the patient's symptoms and character problems, and interprets them for the patient to create insight for resolution of the problems.

The specifics of the analyst's interventions typically include confronting and clarifying the patient's pathological defenses, wishes and guilt. Through the analysis of conflicts, including those contributing to resistance and those involving transference onto the analyst of distorted reactions, psychoanalytic treatment can clarify how patients unconsciously are their own worst enemies: how unconscious, symbolic reactions that have been stimulated by experience are causing symptoms.

Short History of Psychoanalysis

1890s

The idea of psychoanalysis was developed in Vienna in the 1890s by Sigmund Freud, a neurologist interested in finding an effective treatment for patients with neurotic or hysterical symptoms. Freud had become aware of the existence of mental processes that were not conscious as a result of his neurological consulting job at the Children's Hospital, where he noticed that many aphasic children had no organic cause for their symptoms. He wrote a monograph about this subject. In the late 1880s, Freud obtained a grant to study with Jean-Martin Charcot, the famed neurologist and syphilologist, at the Salpêtrière in Paris. Charcot had become interested in patients who had symptoms that mimicked general paresis. Freud's first theory to explain hysterical symptoms was the so-called "seduction theory". Since his patients under treatment with this new method "remembered" incidents of having been sexually seduced in childhood, Freud believed that they had actually been abused only to later repress those memories. This led to his publication with Dr. Breuer in 1893 of case reports of the treatment of hysteria. This first theory became untenable as an explanation of all incidents of hysteria. As a result of his work with his patients, Freud learned that the majority complained of sexual problems, especially coitus interruptus as birth control. He suspected their problems stemmed from cultural restrictions on sexual expression and that their sexual wishes and fantasies had been repressed. Between this discovery of the unexpressed sexual desires and the relief of the symptoms by abreaction, Freud began to theorize that the unconscious mind had determining effects on hysterical symptoms.

His first comprehensive attempt at an explanatory theory was the then unpublished Project for a Scientific Psychology in 1895. In this work Freud attempted to develop a neurophysiologic theory based on transfer of energy by the neurons in the brain in order to explain unconscious mechanisms. He abandoned the project when he came to realize that there was a complicated psychological process involved over and above neuronal activity. By 1900, Freud had discovered that dreams had symbolic significance, and generally were specific to the dreamer. Freud formulated his second psychological theory - which postulates that the unconscious has or is a "primary process" consisting of symbolic and condensed thoughts, and a "secondary process" of logical, conscious thoughts. This theory was published in his 1900 opus magnum, "The Interpretation of Dreams". Chapter VII was a re-working of the earlier "Project" and Freud outlined his "Topographic Theory." In this theory, which was mostly later supplanted by the Structural Theory, unacceptable sexual wishes were repressed into the "System Unconscious," unconscious due to society's condemnation of premarital sexual activity, and this repression created anxiety. Freud also discovered what most of us take for granted today: that dreams were symbolic and specific to the dreamer. Often, dreams give clues to unconscious conflicts, and for this reason, Freud referred to dreams as the "royal road to the Unconscious."

1900–1940s

This "topographic theory" is still popular in much of Europe, although it has been superseded in much of North America. In 1905, Freud published Three Essays on the Theory of Sexuality in which he laid out his discovery of so-called psychosexual phases: oral (ages 0–2), anal (2-4), phallic-oedipal (today called 1st genital) (3-6), latency (6-puberty), and mature genital (puberty-onward). His early formulation included the idea that because of societal restrictions, sexual wishes were repressed into an unconscious state, and that the energy of these unconscious wishes could be turned into anxiety or physical symptoms. Therefore the early treatment techniques, including hypnotism and abreaction, were designed to make the unconscious conscious in order to relieve the pressure and the apparently resulting symptoms.

In "On Narcissism" (1915) Freud turned his attention to the subject of narcissism. Still utilizing an energic system, Freud conceptualized the question of energy directed at the self versus energy directed at others, called cathexis. By 1917, In "Mourning and Melancholia," he suggested that certain depressions were caused by turning guilt-ridden anger on the self. In 1919 in "A Child is Being Beaten", he began to address the problems of self-destructive behavior (moral masochism) and frank sexual masochism. Based on his experience with depressed and self-destructive patients, and pondering the carnage of WWI, Freud became dissatisfied with considering only oral and sexual motivations for behavior. By 1920, Freud addressed the power of identification (with the leader and with other members) in groups as a motivation for behavior (Group Psychology and Analysis of the Ego). In that same year (1920) Freud suggested his "dual drive" theory of sexuality and aggression in Beyond the Pleasure Principle, to try to begin to explain human destructiveness.

In 1923, he presented his new "structural theory" of an id, ego, and superego in a book entitled, "The Ego and the Id". Therein, he revised the whole theory of mental functioning, now considering that repression was only one of many defense mechanisms, and that it occurred to reduce anxiety. Note that repression, for Freud, is both a cause of anxiety and a response to anxiety. In 1926, in "Inhibitions, Symptoms and Anxiety", Freud laid out how intrapsychic conflict among drive and superego (wishes and guilt) caused anxiety, and how that anxiety could lead to an inhibition of mental functions, such as intellect and speech. "Inhibitions, Symptoms and Anxiety" was written in response to Otto Rank, who, in 1924, published "Das Trauma der Geburt" (translated into English in 1929 as "The Trauma of Birth"), exploring how art, myth, religion, philosophy and therapy were illuminated by separation anxiety in the "phase before the development of the Oedipus complex". But there was no such phase in Freud's theories. The Oedipus complex, Freud explained tirelessly, was the nucleus of the neurosis and the foundational source of all art, myth, religion, philosophy, therapy—indeed of all human culture and civilization. It was the first time that anyone in the inner circle had dared to suggest that the Oedipus complex might not be the only factor contributing to intrapsychic

41

development

By 1936, the "Principle of Multiple Function" was clarified by Robert Waelder. He widened the formulation that psychological symptoms were caused by and relieved conflict simultaneously. Moreover, symptoms (such as phobias and compulsions) each represented elements of some drive wish (sexual and/or aggressive), superego (guilt), anxiety, reality, and defenses. Also in 1936, Anna Freud, Sigmund's famous daughter, published her seminal book, "The Ego and the Mechanisms of Defense", outlining numerous ways the mind could shut upsetting things out of consciousness.

1940s-2000s

Following the death of Freud, a new group of psychoanalysts began to explore the function of the ego. Led by Hartmann, Kris, Rappaport and Lowenstein, the group built upon understandings of the synthetic function of the ego as a mediator in psychic functioning. Hartmann, in particular, distinguished between autonomous ego functions (such as memory and intellect which could be secondarily affected by conflict) and synthetic functions which were a result of compromise formation. These "Ego Psychologists" of the '50s paved a way to focus analytic work by attending to the defenses (mediated by the ego) before exploring the deeper roots to the unconscious conflicts. In addition there was burgeoning interest in child psychoanalysis. Although criticized since its inception, psychoanalysis has been used as a research tool into childhood development, and has is still used to treat certain mental disturbances. In the 1960s, Freud's early thoughts on the childhood development of female sexuality were challenged; this challenge led to the development of a variety of understandings of female sexual development, many of which modified the timing and normality of several of Freud's theories (which had been gleaned from the treatment of women with mental disturbances). Several researchers followed Karen Horney's studies of societal pressures that influence the development of women. Most contemporary North American psychoanalysts employ theories that, while based on those of Sigmund Freud, include many modifications of theory and practice developed since his death in 1939.

In 2000, there were approximately 35 training institutes for psychoanalysis in the United States accredited by the American Psychoanalytic Association, which is a component organization of the International Psychoanalytical Association, and there are over 3,000 graduated psychoanalysts practicing in the United States. The International

Psychoanalytical Association accredits psychoanalytic training centers throughout the rest of the world, including countries such as Serbia, France, Germany, Austria, Italy, Switzerland, and many others, as well as about six institutes directly in the U.S. Freud published a paper entitled "The History of the Psychoanalytic Movement" in 1914, German original being first published in the Jahrbuch der Psychoanalyse.

Variations of Psychoanalytic Theories

The predominant psychoanalytic theories can be grouped into several theoretical "schools." Although these theoretical "schools" differ, most of them continue to stress the strong influence of unconscious elements affecting people's mental lives. There has also been considerable work done on consolidating elements of Conflicting Theory - the works of Theodore Dorpat, B. Killingmo, and S. Akhtar. As in all fields of healthcare, there are some persistent conflicts regarding specific causes of some syndromes, and disputes regarding the best treatment techniques. In the 2000s, psychoanalytic ideas are embedded in Western culture, especially in fields such as childcare, education, literary criticism, cultural studies, and mental health, particularly psychotherapy. Though there is a mainstream of evolved analytic ideas, there are groups who follow the precepts of one or more of the later theoreticians. Psychoanalytic ideas also play roles in some types of literary analysis such as Archetypal literary criticism.

Interpersonal Psychoanalysis

Interpersonal psychoanalysis accents the nuances of interpersonal interactions, particularly how individuals protect themselves from anxiety by establishing collusive interactions with others, and the relevance of actual experiences with other persons developmentally (e.g. family and peers) as well as in the present. This is contrasted with the primacy of intrapsychic forces, as in classical psychoanalysis. Interpersonal theory was first introduced by Harry Stack Sullivan, MD, and developed further by Frieda Fromm-Reichmann, Clara Thompson, Erich Fromm, and others who contributed to the founding of the William Alanson White Institute and Interpersonal Psychoanalysis in general.

Childhood Origins

Freudian theories point out that adult problems can be traced to unresolved conflicts from certain phases of childhood and adolescence. Freud, based on the data gathered from his patients early in his career, suspected that neurotic disturbances occurred when children were sexually abused in childhood (the so-called seduction theory). Later, Freud came to believe that, although child abuse occurs, not all neurotic symptoms were associated with this. He realized that neurotic people often had unconscious conflicts that involved incestuous fantasies deriving from different stages of development. He found the stage from about three to six years of age (preschool years, today called the "first genital stage") to be filled with fantasies of having romantic relationships with both parents. Although arguments were generated in early 20th-century Vienna about whether adult seduction of children was the basis of neurotic illness, there is virtually no argument about this problem in the 21st century.

Many psychoanalysts who work with children have studied the actual effects of child abuse, which include ego and object relations deficits and severe neurotic conflicts. Much research has been done on these types of trauma in childhood, and the adult sequelae of those. On the other hand, many adults with symptom neuroses and character pathology have no history of childhood sexual or physical abuse. In studying the childhood factors that start neurotic symptom development, Freud found a constellation of factors that, for literary reasons, he termed the Oedipus complex based on the play by Sophocles, Oedipus Rex, where the protagonist unwittingly kills his father Laius and marries his mother Jocasta. The shorthand term, "Oedipal," Sandler-1960 and modified by Charles Brenner in 1982 refers to the powerful attachments that children make to their parents in the preschool years. These attachments involve fantasies of sexual relationships with either, or both, parent, and, therefore, competitive fantasies toward either, or both, parents. Humberto Nagera (1975) has been particularly helpful in clarifying many of the complexities of the child through these years.

The terms "positive" and "negative" oedipal conflicts have been attached to the heterosexual and homosexual aspects, respectively. Both seem to occur in development of most children. Eventually, the developing child's concessions to reality - that they will neither marry one parent nor eliminate the other - lead to identifications with parental values. These identifications generally create a new set of mental operations regarding values and guilt, subsumed under the term "superego." Besides superego development, children "resolve" their preschool oedipal conflicts through channeling wishes into something their parents approve of ("sublimation") and the development, during the school-age years ("latency") of age-appropriate obsessive-compulsive defensive maneuvers (rules, repetitive games).

Types of Treatment

Using the various analytic theories to assess mental problems, several particular constellations of problems are particularly suited for analytic techniques whereas other problems respond better to medicines and different interpersonal interventions. To be treated with psychoanalysis, whatever the presenting problem, the person requesting help must demonstrate a desire to start an analysis. The person wishing to start an analysis must have some capacity for speech and communication. As well, they need to be able to have trust and empathy within the psychoanalytic session. Potential patients must undergo a preliminary stage of treatment to assess their amenability to psychoanalysis, at that time, and also to enable the analyst to form a working psychological model that the analyst will use to direct the treatment. Psychoanalysts mainly work with neurosis and hysteria in particular, however adapted forms of psychoanalysis are used in working with schizophrenia and other forms of psychosis. Finally, if a prospective patient is severely suicidal a longer preliminary stage may be employed, sometimes with sessions that have a twenty-minute break in the middle. There are modifications of techniques due to the radically individualistic nature of each person's analysis.

The most common problems treatable with psychoanalysis include: phobias, conversions, compulsions, obsessions, anxiety attacks, depressions, sexual dysfunctions, a wide variety of relationship problems (such as dating and marital strife), and a wide variety of character problems (for example, painful shyness, meanness, obnoxiousness, workaholism, hyperseductiveness, hyperemotionality, hyperfastidiousness). The fact that many of such patients also demonstrate deficits above makes diagnosis and treatment selection difficult.

Analytical organizations such as the International Psychoanalytic Association, The American Psychoanalytic Association, and the European Federation for Psychoanalytic Psychotherapy, have established procedures and models for the indication and practice of psychoanalytical therapy for trainees in analysis. The match between the analyst and the patient can be viewed as another contributing factor for the indication and contraindication

45

for psychoanalytic treatment. The analyst decides whether the patient is suitable for psychoanalysis. This decision made by the analyst, besides made on the usual indications and pathology, is also based to a certain degree by the "fit" between analyst and patient. A person's suitability for analysis at any particular time is based on their desire to know something about where their illness has come from. Someone who is not suitable for analysis expresses no desire to know more about the root causes of their illness. An evaluation may include one or more other analysts' independent opinions and will include discussion of the patient's financial situation and insurances.

Techniques

The basic method of psychoanalysis is interpretation of the patient's unconscious conflicts that are interfering with current-day functioning – conflicts that are causing painful symptoms such as phobias, anxiety, depression, and compulsions. Strachey (1936) stressed that figuring out ways the patient distorted perceptions about the analyst led to understanding what may have been forgotten. In particular, unconscious hostile feelings toward the analyst could be found in symbolic, negative reactions to what Robert Langs later called the "frame" of the therapy – the setup that included times of the sessions, payment of fees, and necessity of talking. In patients who made mistakes, forgot, or showed other peculiarities regarding time, fees, and talking, the analyst can usually find various unconscious "resistances" to the flow of thoughts (sometimes called free association).

Freud's patients would lie on this couch during psychoanalysis with patient reclines on a couch with the analyst out of view, the patient tends to remember more, experience more resistance and transference, and be able to reorganize thoughts after the development of insight – through the interpretive work of the analyst. Although fantasy life can be understood through the examination of dreams, masturbation fantasies (cf. Marcus, I. and Francis, J. (1975), "Masturbation from Infancy to Senescence" are also important. The analyst is interested in how the patient reacts to and avoids such fantasies (cf. Paul Gray (1994), "The Ego and the Analysis of Defense". Various memories of early life are generally distorted – Freud called them "screen memories" – and in any case, very early experiences (before age two) – cannot be remembered.

Cost and length of treatment

The cost to the patient of psychoanalytic treatment ranges widely from place to place and between practitioners. Since, in most locations in the United States, unlike in Ontario and Germany, classical analysis (which usually requires sessions three to five times per week) is not covered by health insurance, many analysts may negotiate their fees with patients whom they feel they can help, but who have financial difficulties. The modifications of analysis, which include dynamic therapy, brief therapies, and certain types of group therapy, are carried out on a less frequent basis - usually once, twice, or three times a week - and usually the patient sits facing the therapist.

Many studies have also been done on briefer "dynamic" treatments; these are more expedient to measure, and shed light on the therapeutic process to some extent. Brief Relational Therapy (BRT), Brief Psychodynamic Therapy (BPT), and Time-Limited Dynamic Therapy (TLDP) limit treatment to 20-30 sessions. On average, classical analysis may last 5.7 years, but for phobias and depressions uncomplicated by ego deficits or object relations deficits, analysis may run for a shorter period of time. Longer analyses are indicated for those with more serious disturbances in object relations, more symptoms, and more ingrained character pathology (such as obnoxiousness, severe passivity, or heinous procrastination).

Training and Research

Psychoanalytic training in the United States, in most locations, involves personal analytic treatment for the trainee, conducted confidentially, with no report to the Education Committee of the Analytic Training Institute; approximately 600 hours of class instruction, with a standard curriculum, over a four-year period. Classes are often a few hours per week, or for a full day or two every other weekend during the academic year; this varies with the institute; and supervision once per week, with a senior analyst, on each analytic treatment case the trainee has. Male and female cases are required. Supervision must go on for at least a few years on one or more cases. Supervision is done in the supervisor's office, where the trainee presents material from the analytic work that week, examines the unconscious conflicts with the supervisor, and learns, discusses, and is advised about technique.

Many psychoanalytic Training Centers in the United States have been accredited by special committees of the American Psychoanalytic Association or the International Psychoanalytical Association. Because of theoretical differences, other independent institutes arose, usually founded by psychologists, who until 1987 were not permitted access to psychoanalytic training institutes of the American Psychoanalytic Association. Currently there are between seventy-five and one hundred independent institutes in the United States. As well, other institutes are affiliated to other organizations such as the American Academy of Psychoanalysis and Dynamic Psychiatry, and the National Association for the Advancement of Psychoanalysis. At most psychoanalytic institutes in the United States, qualifications for entry include a terminal degree in a mental health field, such as Ph.D., Psy.D., M.S.W., or M.D. A few institutes restrict applicants to those already holding an M.D. or Ph.D., and most institutes in Southern California confer a Ph.D. or Psy.D. in psychoanalysis upon graduation, which involves completion of the necessary requirements for the state boards that confer that doctoral degree. The first training institute in America to educate non-medical psychoanalysts was The National Psychological Association for Psychoanalysis., (1978) in New York City. It was founded by the world famous analyst Theodor Reik.

The International Psychoanalytical Association (IPA) is the world's primary accrediting and regulatory body for psychoanalysis. The Division of Psychoanalysis of the American Psychological Association (APA) was established in the early 1980s by several psychologists, principal among them were Ruben Fine, Ph.D., Robert C. Lane. Ph.D., Max Rosenbaum, Ph.D. Nathan Stockhamer, Ph.D, Helen Block Lewis, Ph.D. and George Goldman, Ph.D. Until the establishment of the Division of Psychoanalysis, psychologists who had trained in independent institutes had no national organization.

Adlerian Therapy

Alfred Adler (February 7, 1870 – May 28, 1937) was an Austrian medical doctor, psychologist and founder of the school of individual psychology. In collaboration with Sigmund Freud and a small group of Freud's colleagues, Adler was among the co-founders of the psychoanalytic movement as a core member of the Vienna Psychoanalytic Society. He was the first major figure to break away from psychoanalysis to form an independent school of psychotherapy and personality theory. This was after Freud declared Adler's ideas as too contrary, leading to an ultimatum to all members of the Society (which Freud had shepherded) to drop Adler or be expelled, disavowing the right to dissent (Makari, 2008). Following this split, Adler would come to have an enormous, independent effect on the disciplines of counseling and psychotherapy as they developed over the course of the 20th century (Ellenberger, 1970). He influenced notable figures in subsequent schools of psychotherapy such as Rollo May, Viktor Frankl, Abraham Maslow and Albert Ellis. His writings preceded, and were at times surprisingly consistent with, later neo-Freudian insights such as those evidenced in the works of Karen Horney, Harry Stack Sullivan and Erich Fromm.

Adler emphasized the importance of equality in preventing various forms of psychopathology, and espoused the development of social interest and democratic family structures for raising children. His most famous concept is the inferiority complex which speaks to the problem of self-esteem and its negative effects on human health (e.g. sometimes producing a paradoxical superiority striving). His emphasis on power dynamics is rooted in the philosophy of Nietzsche. Adler argued for holism, viewing the individual holistically rather than reductively, the latter being the dominant lens for viewing human psychology. Adler was also among the first in psychology to argue in favor of feminism making the case that power dynamics between men and women (and associations with masculinity and femininity) are crucial to understanding human psychology (Connell, 1995). Adler is considered, along with Freud and Jung, to be one of the three founding figures of depth psychology, which emphasizes the unconscious and psychodynamics (Ellenberger, 1970; Ehrenwald, 1991).

Basic principles

Adler was influenced by the mental construct ideas of the philosopher Hans Vaihinger (The Philosophy of As If / Philosophie des Als Ob) and the literature of Dostoevsky. While still a member of the Vienna Psychoanalytic Society he developed a theory of organic inferiority and compensation that was the prototype for his later turn to phenomenology and the development of his famous concept, the inferiority complex.

Adler was also influenced by the philosophies of Immanuel Kant, Friedrich Nietzsche, Rudolf Virchow and the statesman Jan Smuts (who coined the term "holism"). Adler's School, known as "Individual Psychology" - an arcane reference to the Latin individuus meaning indivisibility, a term intended to emphasize holism - is both a social and community psychology as well as a depth psychology. Adler was an early advocate in psychology for prevention and emphasized the training of parents, teachers, social workers and so on in democratic approaches that allow a child to exercise their power through reasoned decision making whilst cooperating with others. He was a social idealist, and was known as a socialist in his early years of association with psychoanalysis (1902–1911). His allegiance to Marxism dissipated over time (he retained Marx's social idealism yet distanced himself from Marx's economic theories).

Adler (1938) was a very pragmatic man and believed that lay people could make practical use of the insights of psychology. He sought to construct a social movement united under the principles of "Gemeinschaftsgefuehl" (community feeling) and social interest (the practical actions that are exercised for the social good). Adler was also an early supporter of feminism in psychology and the social world, believing that feelings of superiority and inferiority were often gendered and expressed symptomatically in characteristic masculine and feminine styles. These styles could form the basis of psychic compensation and lead to mental health difficulties. Adler also spoke of "safeguarding tendencies" and neurotic behavior long before Anna Freud wrote about the same phenomena in her book "The Ego and the Mechanisms of Defense".

Adlerian-based scholarly, clinical and social practices focus on the following topics:

> Mental Health Prevention
> Social Interest and Community Feeling
> Holism and the Creative Self
> Fictional Finalism, Teleology, and Goal constructs
> Psychological and Social Encouragement
> Inferiority, Superiority and Compensation
> Life Style / Style of Life
> Early Recollections (a projective technique)
> Family Constellation and Birth Order
> Life Tasks & Social Embeddedness
> The Conscious and Unconscious realms
> Private Logic & Common Sense (based in part on Kant's "sensus
>   communis")
> Symptoms and Neurosis
> Safeguarding Behaviour

Guilt and Guilt Feelings
Socratic Questioning
Dream Interpretation
Child and Adolescent Psychology
Democratic approaches to Parenting and Families
Leadership and Organizational Psychology

From its inception, Adlerian psychology has always included both professional and lay adherents. Indeed, Adler felt that all people could make use of the scientific insights garnered by psychology and he welcomed everyone, from decorated academics to those with no formal education to participate in spreading the principles of Adlerian psychology.

Adler's approach to Personality

Adler's book, "Über den nervösen Charakter" (The Neurotic Character) defines his earlier key ideas. He argued that human personality could be explained teleologically, parts of the individual's unconscious self-ideal work to convert feelings of inferiority to superiority (or rather completeness). The desires of the self-ideal were countered by social and ethical demands. If the corrective factors were disregarded and the individual over-compensated, then an inferiority complex would occur, fostering the danger of the individual becoming egocentric, power-hungry and aggressive or worse. Common therapeutic tools include the use of humor, historical instances, and paradoxical injunctions.

Psychodynamics and Teleology

Adler maintained that human psychology is **psychodynamic** in nature, yet unlike Freud's metapsychology that emphasizes instinctual demands, human psychology is guided by goals and fueled by a yet unknown creative force. Like Freud's instincts, Adler's fictive goals are largely unconscious. These goals have a "teleological" function. Constructivist Adlerians, influenced by neo-Kantian and Nietzschean ideas, view these "teleological" goals as "fictions" in the sense that Hans Vaihinger spoke of fictio. Usually there is a fictional final goal that can be deciphered alongside of innumerable sub-goals. The inferiority/superiority dynamic is constantly at work through various forms of compensation and over-compensation. For example, in anorexia nervosa the fictive final goal is to "be perfectly thin" (overcompensation on the basis of a feeling of inferiority). Hence, the fictive final goal can serve a persecutory function that is ever-present in subjectivity (though its trace springs are usually unconscious). The end goal of being "thin" is fictive however since it can never be subjectively achieved.

Teleology serves another vital function for Adlerians. Chilon's "hora telos" ("see the end, consider the consequences") provides for both healthy and maladaptive psychodynamics. Here we also find Adler's emphasis on personal responsibility in mentally healthy subjects who seek their own and the social good (Slavik & King, 2007).

Constructivism and metaphysics

The metaphysical thread of Adlerian theory does not problematize the notion of teleology since concepts such as eternity (an ungraspable end where time ceases to exist) match the religious aspects that are held in tandem. In contrast, the constructivist Adlerian threads (either humanist/modernist or postmodern in variant) seek to raise insight of the force of unconscious fictions – which carry all of the inevitability of "fate" – so long as one does not understand them. Here, "teleology" itself is fictive yet experienced as quite real. This aspect of Adler's theory is somewhat analogous to the principles developed in Rational Emotive Behavior Therapy (REBT) and Cognitive Therapy (CT). Both Albert Ellis and Aaron T. Beck credit Adler as a major precursor to REBT and CT. Ellis in particular was a member of the North American Society for Adlerian Psychology and served as an editorial board member for the Adlerian Journal Individual Psychology.

As a psychodynamic system, Adlerians excavate the past of a client/patient in order to alter their future and increase integration into community in the "here-and-now". The 'here-and-now' aspects are especially relevant to those Adlerians who emphasize humanism and/or existentialism in their approaches. It also changes the way of how we look at life.

Holism

Metaphysical Adlerians emphasize a spiritual holism in keeping with what Jan Smuts articulated (Smuts coined the term "holism"), that is, the spiritual sense of one-ness that holism usually implies (holism: from holos, a Greek word meaning all, entire, total). Smuts believed that evolution involves a progressive series of lesser wholes integrating into larger ones. Whilst Smuts' text "Holism and Evolution" is thought to be a work of science, it actually attempts to unify evolution with a higher metaphysical principle (holism). The sense of connection and one-ness revered in various religious traditions (among these, Baha'i, Christianity, Judaism, Islam and Buddhism) finds a strong complement in Adler's thought.

The pragmatic and materialist aspects to contextualizing members of communities, the construction of communities and the socio-historical-political forces that shape communities matter a great deal when it comes to understanding an individual's psychological make-up and functioning. This aspect of Adlerian psychology holds a high level of synergy with the field of community psychology. However, Adlerian psychology, unlike community psychology, is holistically concerned with both prevention and clinical treatment after-the-fact. Hence, Adler cannot be considered the "first community psychologist".

Adlerian psychology, Carl Jung's Analytical Psychology, Gestalt Therapy and Karen Horney's psychodynamic approach are holistic schools of psychology. These discourses eschew a reductive approach to understanding human psychology and psychopathology.

Typology

Adler developed a scheme of so-called personality types. These types are to be taken as provisional or heuristic since he did not, in essence, believe in personality types. The danger with typology is to lose sight of the individual's uniqueness and to gaze reductively, acts that Adler opposed. Nevertheless, he intended to illustrate patterns that could denote a characteristic governed under the overall style of life. American Adlerians have made use of Adler's typology in this provisional sense:

The Getting or Leaning type are those who selfishly take without giving back. These people also tend to be antisocial and have low activity levels.

The Avoiding types are those that hate being defeated. They may be successful, but have not taken any risks getting there. They are likely to have low social contact in fear of rejection or defeat in any way.

The Ruling or Dominant type strive for power and are willing to manipulate situations and people, anything to get their way. People of this type are also prone to anti-social behavior.

The Socially Useful types are those who are very outgoing and very active. They have a lot of social contact and strive to make changes for the good. These "types" are typically formed in childhood and are expressions of the Style of Life.

Birth Order

Adler often emphasized one's birth order as having an influence on the Style of Life and the strengths and weaknesses in one's psychological make up. Birth Order referred to the placement of siblings within the family. Adler believed that the firstborn child would be loved and nurtured by the family until the arrival of a second child. This second child would cause the first born to suffer feelings of dethronement, no longer being the center of attention. Adler believed that in a three-child family, the oldest child would be the most likely to suffer from neuroticism and substance addiction which he reasoned was a compensation for the feelings of excessive responsibility "the weight of the world on one's shoulders" (e.g. having to look after the younger ones) and the melancholic loss of that once supremely pampered position. As a result, he predicted that this child was the most likely to end up in jail or an asylum. Youngest children would tend to be overindulged, leading to poor social empathy. Consequently, the middle child, who would experience neither dethronement nor overindulgence, was most likely to develop into a successful individual yet also most likely to be a rebel and to feel squeezed-out. Adler himself was the second in a family of six children.

Adler never produced any scientific support for his interpretations on birth order roles. Yet the value of the hypothesis was to extend the importance of siblings in marking the psychology of the individual beyond Freud's more limited emphasis on the Mother and Father. Hence, Adlerians spend time therapeutically mapping the influence that siblings (or lack thereof) had on the psychology of their clients. The idiographic approach entails an excavation of the phenomenology of one's birth order position for likely influence on the subject's Style of Life. In sum, the subjective experiences of sibling positionality and inter-relations are psychodynamically important for Adlerian therapists and personality theorists, not the cookbook predictions that may or may not have been objectively true in Adler's time.

Client Centered Therapy

Client Centered Therapy is an approach to counseling and psychotherapy that places much of the responsibility for the treatment process on the patient, with the therapist taking a non-directive role.

Developed in the 1930s by the American psychologist Carl Rogers, client-centered therapy—also known as non-directive or Rogerian therapy—departed from the typically formal, detached role of the therapist common to psychoanalysis and other forms of treatment. Rogers believed that therapy should take place in the supportive environment created by a close personal relationship between client and therapist. Rogers's introduction of the term "client" rather than "patient" expresses his rejection of the traditionally authoritarian relationship between therapist and client and his view of them as equals. The client determines the general direction of therapy, while the therapist seeks to increase the client's insightful self-understanding through informal clarifying questions.

Rogers believed that the most important factor in successful therapy was not the therapist's skill or training, but rather his or her attitude. Three interrelated attitudes on the part of the therapist are central to the success of client-centered therapy: congruence, unconditional positive regard, and empathy. Congruence refers to the therapist's openness and genuineness—the willingness to relate to clients without hiding behind a professional facade. Therapists who function in this way have all their feelings available to them in therapy sessions and may share significant ones with their clients. However, congruence does not mean that therapists disclose their own personal problems to clients in therapy sessions or shift the focus of therapy to themselves in any other way.

Unconditional positive regard means that the therapist accepts the client totally for who he or she is without evaluating or censoring, and without disapproving of particular feelings, actions, or characteristics. The therapist communicates this attitude to the client by a willingness to listen without interrupting, judging, or giving advice. This creates a nonthreatening context in which the client feels free to explore and share painful, hostile, defensive, or abnormal feelings without worrying about personal rejection by the therapist.

The third necessary component of a therapist's attitude is empathy ("accurate empathetic understanding"). The therapist tries to appreciate the client's situation from the client's point of view, showing an emotional understanding of and sensitivity to the client's feelings throughout the therapy session. In other systems of therapy, empathy with the client would be considered a preliminary step enabling the therapeutic work to proceed, but in client-centered therapy, it actually constitutes a major portion of the therapeutic work itself. A primary way of conveying this empathy is by active listening that shows careful and perceptive attention to what the client is saying. In addition to standard techniques, such as eye contact, that are common to any good listener, client-centered therapists employ a special method called reflection, which consists of paraphrasing and/or summarizing what a client has just said. This technique shows that the therapist is listening carefully and accurately and gives clients an added opportunity to examine their own thoughts and feelings as they hear them repeated by another person. Generally, clients respond by elaborating further on the thoughts they have just expressed.

Two primary goals of client-centered therapy are increased self-esteem and greater openness to experience. Some of the related changes that it seeks to foster in clients include increased correspondence between the client's idealized and actual selves; better self-understanding; decreases in defensiveness, guilt, and insecurity; more positive and comfortable relationships with others; and an increased capacity to experience and express feelings at the moment they occur. Beginning in the 1960s, client-centered therapy became allied with the human potential movement. Rogers adopted terms such as "person-centered approach" and "way of being" and began to focus on personal growth and self-actualization. He also pioneered the use of encounter groups, adapting the sensitivity training (T-group) methods developed by Kurt Lewin (1890-1947) and other researchers at the National Training Laboratories in 1950s.

While **client-centered therapy** is considered one of the major therapeutic approaches, along with psychoanalytic and cognitive-behavioral therapy, Rogers' influence is felt in schools of therapy other than his own, and the concepts and methods he developed are drawn on in an eclectic fashion by many different types of counselors and therapists.

QUALITIES OF THE THERAPIST

Congruence: therapist's openness to the client

Unconditional positive regard: therapist accepts the client without judgment

Empathy: therapist tries to convey an appreciation and understanding of the client's point of view

GOALS OF THE THERAPY

Increase self-esteem

Expand openness to life experiences.

Gestalt Therapy

Gestalt therapy as "a conceptual and methodological base from which helping professionals can craft their practice". In the same volume Joel Latner stated that Gestalt therapy is built upon two central ideas: that the most helpful focus of psychotherapy is the experiential present moment, and that everyone is caught in webs of relationships; thus, it is only possible to know ourselves against the background of our relationship to the other. The historical development of Gestalt therapy (described below) discloses the influences that generated these two ideas. Expanded, they support the four chief theoretical constructs (explained in the theory and practice section) that comprise Gestalt theory, and that guide the practice and application of Gestalt therapy.

Gestalt therapy was forged from various influences upon the lives of its founders during the times in which they lived, including: the new physics, Eastern religion, existential phenomenology, Gestalt psychology, psychoanalysis, experimental theatre, as well as systems theory and field theory. Gestalt therapy rose from its beginnings in the middle of the 20th century to rapid and widespread popularity during the decade of the 1960s and early 1970s. During the '70s and '80s Gestalt therapy training centers spread globally; but they were, for the most part, not aligned with formal academic settings. As the cognitive revolution eclipsed Gestalt theory in psychology, many came to believe Gestalt was an anachronism. Gestalt therapy became merely an applied discipline in the fields of organizational development, social action, and eventually coaching. Gestalt therapists disdained the positivism underlying what they perceived to be the concern of research, and so they largely ignored the need to utilize research to further develop Gestalt theory and Gestalt therapy practice. However, the new century has seen a sea of change in attitudes toward research and Gestalt practice.

Gestalt therapy largely focuses on process (what is actually happening) rather than content (what is being talked about). The emphasis is on what is being done, thought, and felt at the present moment (the phenomenality of both client and therapist), rather than on what was, might be, could be, or should have been. Gestalt therapy is a method of awareness practice (also called "mindfulness" in other clinical domains), by which perceiving, feeling, and acting are understood to be conducive to interpreting, explaining, and conceptualizing (the hermeneutics of experience). This distinction between direct experiences versus indirect or secondary interpretation is developed in the process of therapy. The client learns to become aware of what he or she is doing and that triggers a shift or change.

The objective of Gestalt therapy is to enable the client to become more fully and creatively alive and to become free from the blocks and unfinished business that may diminish satisfaction, fulfillment, and growth. For this reason Gestalt therapy falls within the category of humanistic psychotherapies. Because Gestalt therapy includes perception and the meaning-making processes by which experience forms, it can also be considered a cognitive approach. Because Gestalt therapy relies on the contact between therapist and client, and because a relationship can be considered to be contact over time, Gestalt therapy can be considered a relational or interpersonal approach. Because Gestalt therapy appreciates the larger picture which is the complex situation involving multiple influences in a complex situation, it can be considered a multi-systemic approach. Because the processes of Gestalt therapy are experimental, involving action, Gestalt therapy can be considered both a paradoxical and an experiential approach.

When Gestalt therapy is compared to other clinical domains, a person can find many matches, or points of consilience. "Probably the clearest case of consilience is between gestalt therapy's field perspective and the various organismic and field theories that proliferated in neuroscience, medicine, and physics in the early and mid-20th century. Within social science there is a consilience between gestalt field theory and systems or ecological psychotherapy; between the concept of dialogical relationship and object relations, attachment theory, client-centered therapy and the transference-oriented approaches; between the existential, phenomenological, and hermeneutical aspects of gestalt therapy and the constructivist aspects of cognitive therapy; and between gestalt therapy's commitment to awareness and the natural processes of healing and mindfulness, acceptance and Buddhist techniques adopted by cognitive behavioral therapy."

Contemporary theory and practice

Gestalt therapy theory essentially rests atop four "load-bearing walls": phenomenological method, dialogical relationship, field-theoretical strategies, and experimental freedom. Although all these tenets were present in the early formulation and practice of Gestalt therapy, as described in "Ego,

Hunger and Aggression" (Perls, 1947) and in "Gestalt Therapy, Excitement and Growth in the Human Personality" (Perls, Hefferline, & Goodman, 1951), the early development of Gestalt therapy theory emphasized personal experience and the experiential episodes understood as "safe emergencies" or experiments. Indeed, half of the Perls, Hefferline, and Goodman book consists of such experiments. Later, through the influence of such people as Erving and Miriam Polster, a second theoretical emphasis emerged: namely, contact between self and other, and ultimately the dialogical relationship between therapist and client. Later still, field theory emerged as an emphasis. At various times over the decades, since Gestalt therapy first emerged, one or more of these tenets and the associated constructs that go with them have captured the imagination of those who have continued developing the contemporary theory of Gestalt therapy. Since 1990 the literature focused upon Gestalt therapy has flourished, including the development of several professional Gestalt journals. Along the way, Gestalt therapy theory has also been applied in Organizational Development and Coaching work. And, more recently, Gestalt methods have been combined with meditation practices into a unified program of human development called Gestalt Practice.

Phenomenological Method

The goal of a phenomenological exploration is awareness. This exploration works systematically to reduce the effects of bias through repeated observations and inquiry.

The phenomenological method comprises three steps:
(1) the rule of epoché
(2) the rule of description
(3) the rule of horizontalization.

Applying the rule of epoché one sets aside one's initial biases and prejudices in order to suspend expectations and assumptions. Applying the rule of description, one occupies oneself with describing instead of explaining. Applying the rule of horizontalization one treats each item of description as having equal value or significance.

The rule of epoché sets aside any initial theories with regard to what is presented in the meeting between therapist and client. The rule of description implies immediate and specific observations, abstaining from interpretations or explanations, especially those formed from the application of a clinical theory superimposed over the circumstances of experience. The rule of horizontalization avoids any hierarchical assignment of importance such that the data of experience become prioritized and categorized as they are received. A Gestalt therapist utilizing the phenomenological method might say something like, "I notice a slight tension at the corners of your mouth when I say that, and I see you shifting on the couch and folding your arms across your chest... and now I see you rolling your eyes back". Of course, the therapist may make a clinically relevant evaluation, but when applying the phenomenological method, temporarily suspends the need to express it.

Dialogical relationship

To create the conditions under which a dialogic moment might occur, the therapist attends to his or her own presence, creates the space for the client to enter in and become present as well (called inclusion), and commits him or herself to the dialogic process, surrendering to what takes place, as opposed to attempting to control it. With presence, the therapist "shows up" as a whole and authentic person, instead of assuming a role, false self or persona. To practice inclusion is to accept however the client chooses to be present, whether in a defensive and obnoxious stance or a superficially cooperative one. To practice inclusion is to support the presence of the client, including his or her resistance, not as a gimmick but in full realization that this is how the client is actually present. Finally, a Gestalt therapist is committed to process, following the maxim - trusts process, support process, and get out of the way. From this description one might be hard pressed to envision what a Gestalt therapist really does, or what a session would look like! Since Gestalt therapy is an experiential therapy, it is extremely difficult to summarize it in concepts, like those used here, which Perls probably would have referred to as "elephant shit".

Field-theoretical strategies

"The field" can be considered in two ways. There are ontological dimensions and there are phenomenological dimensions to one's field. The phenomenological dimensions are all those physical and environmental contexts in which we live and move. They might be the office in which one works, the house in which one lives, the city and country of which one is a citizen, and so forth. The ontological field is the objective reality that

60

supports our physical existence. The ontological dimensions are all mental and physical dynamics that contribute to a person's sense of self, one's subjective experience - not merely elements of the environmental context. These might be the memory of an uncle's inappropriate affection, one's color blindness, one's sense of the social matrix in operation at the office in which one works, and so forth. The way that Gestalt therapists choose to work with field dynamics makes what they do strategic. Gestalt therapy focuses upon character structure; according to Gestalt theory, the character structure is dynamic rather than fixed in nature. To become aware of one's character structure, the focus is upon the phenomenological dimensions in the context of the ontological dimensions.

Experimental Freedom

Gestalt therapy is distinct because it moves toward action, away from mere talk therapy, and for this reason is considered an experiential approach. Through experiments, the therapist supports the client's direct experience of something new, instead of merely talking about the possibility of something new. Indeed, the entire therapeutic relationship may be considered experimental, because at one level it is a corrective, relational experience for many clients, and it is a "safe emergency" that is free to turn out however it will. An experiment can also be conceived as a teaching method that creates an experience in which a client might learn something as part of their growth.

Examples might include:
(1) Rather than talking about the client's critical parent, a Gestalt therapist might ask the client to imagine the parent is present, or that the therapist is the parent, and talk to that parent directly
(2) If a client is struggling with how to be assertive, a Gestalt therapist could either (a) have the client say some assertive things to the therapist or members of a therapy group, or (b) give a talk about how one should never be assertive
(3) A Gestalt therapist might notice something about the non-verbal behavior or tone of voice of the client; then the therapist might have the client exaggerate the non-verbal behavior and pay attention to that experience
(4) A Gestalt therapist might work with the breathing or posture of the client, and direct awareness to changes that might happen when the

client talks about different content. With all these experiments the Gestalt therapist is working with process rather than content, the How rather than the What.

Self

In field theory, self is a phenomenological concept, existing in comparison with other. Without the other there is no self, and how I experience the other is inseparable from how I experience the self. The continuity of selfhood (functioning personality) is something that is achieved in relationship, rather than something inherently "inside" the person. This can have its advantages and disadvantages. At one end of the spectrum, I may not have enough self-continuity to be able to make meaningful relationships, or to have a workable sense of who I am. In the middle, my personality is a loose set of ways of being that work for me, including commitments to relationships, work, culture and outlook, always open to change where I need to adapt to new circumstances or just want to try something new. At the other end, my personality is a rigid defensive denial of the new and spontaneous. I act in stereotyped ways, and either induce other people to act in particular and fixed ways towards me; or I redefine their actions to fit with fixed stereotypes.

In Gestalt therapy, the process is not about the self of the client being helped or healed by the fixed self of the therapist, rather it is an exploration of the co-creation of self and other in the here-and-now of the therapy. There is no assumption that the client will act in all other circumstances as he or she does in the therapy situation. However, the areas that cause problems will be either the lack of self-definition leading to chaotic or psychotic behavior, or the rigid self-definition in some area of functioning that denies spontaneity and makes dealing with particular situations impossible. Both of these conditions show up very clearly in the therapy, and can be worked with in the relationship with the therapist.

The experience of the therapist is also very much part of the therapy. Since we co-create our self-other experiences, the way a therapist experiences being with a client is significant information about how the clients experience themselves. The proviso here is that a therapist is not operating from their own fixed responses. This is why Gestalt therapists are required to undertake significant therapy of their own during training.

From the perspective of this theory of self, neurosis can be seen as fixed predictability - a fixed Gestalt - and the process of therapy can be seen as facilitating the client to become unpredictable - more responsive to what is in the client's present environment, rather than responding in a stuck way to past introjects or other learning. If the therapist has expectations of how the client should end up, this defeats the aim of therapy.

Change

In what has now become a "classic" of Gestalt therapy literature, Arnold Beisser described Gestalt's paradoxical theory of change. The paradox is that the more one attempts to be who one is not, the more one remains the same. Conversely, when people identify with their current experience, the conditions of wholeness and growth support change. Put another way, change comes about as a result of "full acceptance of what is, rather than a striving to be different".

History

Fritz Perls was a German-Jewish psychoanalyst who fled Europe with his wife Laura Perls to South Africa in order to escape Nazi oppression. After World War II the couple emigrated to New York City, which had become a center of intellectual, artistic and political experimentation by the late 1940s and early 1950s.

Perls served in the German Army during World War I, and was wounded in the conflict. After the war he was educated as a medical doctor. He became an assistant to Kurt Goldstein, who worked with brain-injured soldiers. Perls went through a psychoanalysis with Wilhelm Reich and became a psychiatrist. Perls assisted Goldstein at Frankfurt University where he met his wife Lore (Laura) Posner, who had earned a doctorate in Gestalt Psychology. They fled Nazi Germany in 1933 and settled in South Africa. Perls established a psychoanalytic training institute and joined the South African armed forces, serving as a military psychiatrist. During these years in South Africa Perls was influenced by Jan Smuts and his ideas about "holism".

In 1936 Fritz Perls attended a psychoanalyst's conference in Marienbad, Czechoslovakia, where he presented a paper on oral resistances, mainly based on Laura Perls' notes on breastfeeding their children. Perls' paper was turned down. Perls did present his paper in 1936, but it met with "deep disapproval". Perls wrote his first book, "Ego, Hunger and Aggression" (1942, 1947), in South Africa, based in part on the rejected paper. It was later re-published in the United States. Laura Perls wrote two chapters of this book, but she was not given adequate recognition for her work.

Existential Therapy

Existential Psychotherapy is a method of therapy that operates on the belief that inner conflict within a person is due to that individual's confrontation with the givens of existence. These givens, as noted by Yalom, are: the inevitability of death, freedom and its attendant responsibility, existential isolation (referring to Phenomenology), and finally meaninglessness. These four givens, also referred to as ultimate concerns, form the body of existential psychotherapy and compose the framework in which a therapist conceptualizes a client's problem in order to develop a method of treatment.

The existential psychotherapist is generally not concerned with the client's past; instead, the emphasis is on the choices to be made in the present and future. The counselor and the client may reflect upon how the client has answered life's questions in the past, but attention ultimately shifts to searching for a new and increased awareness in the present and enabling a new freedom and responsibility to act. The patient can then accept they are not special, and that their existence is simply coincidental, without destiny or fate. By accepting this, they can overcome their anxieties, and instead view life as moments, in which they are fundamentally free.

Four worlds

Existential thinkers seek to avoid restrictive models that categorize or label people. Instead they look for the universals that can be observed cross-culturally. There is no existential personality theory which divides humanity into types or reduces people to part components. Instead there is a description of the different levels of experience and existence with which people are inevitably confronted. The way in which a person is in the world at a particular stage can be charted on this general map of human existence (Binswanger, 1963; Yalom, 1980; van Deurzen, 1984). One can distinguish four basic dimensions of human existence: the physical, the social, the psychological and the spiritual. On each of these dimensions people encounter the world and shape their attitude out of their particular take on their experience. Their orientation towards the world defines their reality. The four dimensions are obviously interwoven and provide a complex four-dimensional force field for their existence. Individuals are stretched between a positive pole of what they aspire to on each dimension and a negative pole of what they fear.

Physical dimension
On the physical dimension (Umwelt) individuals relate to their environment and to the givens of the natural world around them. This includes their attitude to the body they have, to the concrete surroundings they find themselves in, to the climate and the weather, to objects and material possessions, to the bodies of other people, their own bodily needs, to health and illness and to their own mortality. The struggle on this dimension is, in general terms, between the search for domination over the elements and natural law (as in technology, or in sports) and the need to accept the limitations of natural boundaries (as in ecology or old age). While people generally aim for security on this dimension (through health and wealth), much of life brings a gradual disillusionment and realization that such security can only be temporary. Recognizing limitations can bring great release of tension.

Social dimension
On the social dimension (Mitwelt) individuals relate to others as they interact with the public world around them. This dimension includes their response to the culture they live in, as well as to the class and race they belong to (and also those they do not belong to). Attitudes here range from love to hate and from cooperation to competition. The dynamic contradictions can be understood in terms of acceptance versus rejection or belonging versus isolation. Some people prefer to withdraw from the world of others as much as possible. Others blindly chase public acceptance by going along with the rules and fashions of the moment. Otherwise they try to rise above these by becoming trendsetters themselves. By acquiring fame or other forms of power, individuals can attain dominance over others temporarily. Sooner or later, however, everyone is confronted with both failure and aloneness.

Psychological dimension
On the psychological dimension (Eigenwelt) individuals relate to themselves and in this way create a personal world. This dimension includes views about their own character, their past experience and their future possibilities. Contradictions here are often experiences in terms of personal strengths and weaknesses. People search for a sense of identity, a feeling of being substantial and having a self. But inevitably many events will confront them

with evidence to the contrary and plunge them into a state of confusion or disintegration. Activity and passivity are an important polarity here. Self-affirmation and resolution go with the former and surrender and yielding with the latter. Facing the final dissolution of self that comes with personal loss and the facing of death might bring anxiety and confusion to many who have not yet given up their sense of self-importance.

Spiritual dimension

On the spiritual dimension (Überwelt) (van Deurzen, 1984) individuals relate to the unknown and thus create a sense of an ideal world, an ideology and a philosophical outlook. It is here that they find meaning by putting all the pieces of the puzzle together for themselves. For some people this is done by adhering to a religion or other prescriptive worldview, for others it is about discovering or attributing meaning in a more secular or personal way. The contradictions that have to be faced on this dimension are often related to the tension between purpose and absurdity, hope and despair. People create their values in search of something that matters enough to live or die for, something that may even have ultimate and universal validity. Usually the aim is the conquest of a soul, or something that will substantially surpass mortality (as for instance in having contributed something valuable to humankind). Facing the void and the possibility of nothingness are the indispensable counterparts of this quest for the eternal.

Reality Therapy

Reality therapy is an approach to psychotherapy and counseling. It was developed by the psychiatrist Dr. William Glasser in 1965. Reality therapy is a considered a cognitive-behavioral approach to treatment. The reality therapy approach to counseling and problem-solving focuses on the here-and-now of the client and how to create a better future. Typically, clients seek to discover what they really want and whether what they are currently doing (how they are choosing to behave) is actually bringing them nearer to, or further away from, that goal.

Reality therapy is more than a counseling technique. Reality therapy is a problem solving method that works well with people who are experiencing problems they want help solving, as well as those who are having problems and appear to not want any assistance. Reality therapy also provides an excellent model for helping individuals solve their own problems objectively and serves as the ideal questioning series during coaching sessions.

The underlying key to reality therapy is the relationship that is established with the person who needs the help. This is most critical when you are attempting to help someone who doesn't really want your help, such as a non-voluntary client, a resistant student or sometimes even your own child. Without a positive relationship, you have no influence.

Reality therapy provides a model of building relationships by instructing helpers to create a need-satisfying counseling environment. The five basic needs of all humans are survival; love and belonging; power; freedom and fun. So, in a helping relationship, the helper must create an environment where it is possible for the person being helped to feel safe; to feel connected to the helper in some way; to be listened to and respected; to have some choices; and to have some fun or learning with the helper. After creating this need-satisfying environment and working hard to maintain it throughout the relationship, the helper can move on to the actual problem.

After hearing the person's story, the helper needs to determine what the ideal solution would look like from the other person's point of view. So, for example, if the person were complaining about a fight he had with his girlfriend, ask the question, "What do you want to happen? How do you want this to work out?" It is critical to get a specific picture of what the ideal solution will look like from the perspective of the person experiencing the problem. The helper is leading him or her away from the problem and into a problem-solution mode. In this way, the focus is off the past and the problem, which cannot be changed. The focus instead is on the behavior the person can create to move himself in the direction of the solution he wants.

The next step is to take an inventory of all the things the person is doing to get the situation to work out the way they want. The helper asks the person to list the steps they're taking to reach their goal. Typically, the person will only list positive things, but the helper must ask them to consider everything that is both helping and hindering progress. The helper may add observations of their own. The point is to get as complete a picture as possible. In addition to considering one's outward behavior, ask about their thoughts, feelings and physiology (if appropriate), as well.

The next step is the most crucial in the entire process. The helper asks helpees if their current behavior is likely to get them what they say they want. If the person is already aware what they're doing is not working, they're already in distress and ready to try something different. The helper assists the client by helping them find a solution.

On the other hand, if the person is unaware they need help, this self-evaluation step helps the client evaluate their behavior and recognize the need to do things differently. It generally creates enough discomfort to at least look at alternatives.

The final step in the reality therapy process is to help the helpee come up with a plan to do something more effective. This is best accomplished by helping the person focus on those things within their control—their own thoughts and actions. We don't help a depressed person by simply saying, "Cheer up!" People cannot directly control their feelings but they can directly control their actions and thinking. Similarly, people like to focus their time and attention on what others could and should do to give them what they want, but attempting to control others is generally a fruitless activity. Helping people to focus on changing their own behavior and thoughts is generally the goal of reality therapy.

Principles
- Focus on the present and avoid discussing the past because all human problems are caused by unsatisfying present relationships.
- Avoid discussing symptoms and complaints as much as possible since these are often the ineffective ways that counselees choose to deal with (and hold on to) unsatisfying relationships.
- Understand the concept of total behavior, which means focus on what counselees can do directly-act and think. Spend less time on what they cannot do directly; that is, changing their feelings and physiology. Feelings and physiology can be changed indirectly, but only if there is a change in the acting and thinking.
- Avoid criticizing, blaming and/or complaining and help counselees to do the same. By doing this, they learn to avoid these extremely harmful external control behaviors that destroy relationships.
- Remain non-judgmental and non-coercive, but encourage people to judge all they are doing by the Choice Theory axiom: Is what I am doing getting me closer to the people I need? If the choice of behaviors is not getting people closer, then the counselor works to help them find new behaviors that lead to a better connection.

- Teach counselees that legitimate or not, excuses stand directly in the way of their making needed connections.
- Focus on specifics. Find out as soon as possible who counselees are disconnected from and work to help them choose reconnecting behaviors. If they are completely disconnected, focus on helping them find a new connection.
- Help them make specific, workable plans to reconnect with the people they need, and then follow through on what was planned by helping them evaluate their progress. Based on their experience, counselors may suggest plans, but should not give the message that there is only one plan. A plan is always open to revision or rejection by the counselee.
- Be patient and supportive but keep focusing on the source of the problem, disconnectedness. Counselees who have been disconnected for a long time will find it difficult to reconnect. They are often so involved in the symptom they are choosing that they have lost sight of the fact that they need to reconnect. Help them to understand, through teaching them Choice Theory and encouraging them to read the book, Choice Theory: A New Psychology of Personal Freedom, that whatever their complaint, reconnecting is the best possible solution to their problem.

When we were little,
we started with the basics of kicking
and punching, then we moved on once
we got proficient in that.
We moved on to working with powerful weapons.
Then after we almost killed everyone,
we decided to go back to the BASICS,
try to figure out WHY
we were fighting and
unhappy in the first place...
Gordon

SECTION III
THERAPIST BASICS

When we work on ourselves, the first thrust is to work on the emotionally painful events that keep us wound up and stressed. In time, we learn to talk about, and to express our feelings, even if there is pain in doing so. By focusing on the cause of our pain and understanding how it has taken us over, eventually we will defuse it, and take back control of our lives. There is a strong comparison, and direct connection, between our physical health and our emotional health. Think of this, when the body experiences a cut or wound, if it is left unattended, it will get infected. Eventually, it will fester and may even turn into gangrene, a life threatening condition. If instead we clean the wound thoroughly, protect it and allow it to heal completely, normally all that would be left is a painless scar to remind us of the situation. No pain, just a blip on the skin.

If we keep emotional wounds in us, and "stuff them" rather than process them, they will fester just like a physical wound and make our lives and us "sick". Emotional stuff kept in, eventually starts to affect other parts of our lives, just as infection would spread to other parts of our body. A certain amount of emotional pain gets experienced routinely, so if a person does not learn to deal appropriately with it, and the feelings, those feelings will build and build and eventually incapacitate you. If, however, the emotional stuff is addressed, and processed, all that is left is a memory. This memory, like an old scar, does not hurt. It can be kept in a safe place in your mind, to be addressed as needed, but does not have to run your life and control it or ruin it and buy you jail time for an aggressive act if you act it out in anger. And remember, often those feelings come out when we have had a "drink or twenty" and our inner control is lacking, so we over react to things, and can find ourselves crying endlessly after a few drinks, or getting angry at the world for how it has treated us.

Often, stress, depression, fear, anxiety and other feelings come out of the blue and we don't know the source. They catch us off guard, but there is a basis for them, a trigger. As a therapist, your role is to help the client to interpret these situations.

• What would make them feel better right now?
• How can they change the way they feel about a situation.
• Remember, you and your client, cannot rewrite history but you can

influence future situations and how they are dealt with.
- Ask yourself, have I lost something? A dream? My support system? A relationship? A family member?
- Ask, what can I do right now that would make me feel less depressed?
- After answering these questions, move to accomplish the things, which you can do to reduce your depression.

Anxiety is often also a source of anger and eepression, as we get anxious about feelings that we don't understand or that bring us down.
- First try to identify your upsetting feelings.
- Usually your upsetting feelings are a signal to slow down, reflect and de-brief.
- Counteract your upsetting thought with a positive self-message.

Anxiety and Depression usually have the same causes, and are really not feelings but a state of feeling, i.e., a state of being. When one is anxious, and it gets out of hand, the body says, "calm down" and throws things into depression, a state of lowered emotions. Same causes, just different state of being.

Stress is the mismatch between the demands made on us and our resources to meet those demands. Stress reduces our capacity to tolerate intense negative feelings such as anger, tears, and hyperactivity.
- When impatience caused by stress appears to be the source of your feelings, consider steps to reduce your stress and your anxiety will likely dissipate.
- Ask yourself, is this a situation I can really change or influence? If the answer is yes, move to take action. If the answer is no, then attempt to develop acceptance skills to reduce the intensity of the feelings.

Miscommunication often leads to hurt feelings, embarrassment, stress, depression, and anger.
- Listen to the other person attentively and allow them the space to either confirm or modify your frame of reference by feeding back to them what you understand the situation to be.
- Use "I" statements and tell the person just what it is that is making

you frustrated, without blaming them and escalating the conflict.

Depression... a Good Sign????

CAN DEPRESSION EVER BE VIEWED AS A GOOD THING?

Recently, I heard a lecturer state that Depression is a good sign. It stopped me in my tracks and started me thinking that there was no way at all that such a negative thing as Depression, that takes so much of our productive life away, and costs so much to treat, could ever be a positive asset.

I was wrong! I was able see how it could apply to my domestic violence batterers' and anger management perpetrators in my groups, as well as other parts of our lives.

HOW DOES DEPRESSION EARN THE TITLE OF <u>A GOOD SIGN</u>?

Go back to our Psych 101 classes and Kubler-Ross' discovery of DABDA. We can remember how Kubler-Ross defined D.A.B.D.A. as a process of stages that people go through in dealing with terminal illnesses but can be applied very well to the stages in a destructive violent relationship, as well as changes in our lives that we avoid as well as to the anger management perpetrator who is sure they never get angry or the alcoholic who "knows when to quit."

DABDA stands for-

D enial
A nger
B argaining
D EPRESSION
A cceptance

We'll use couples who are destined for domestic violence (DV) classes as the sample. Domestic Violence Perpetrators are in **DENIAL** for years that the relationship is either not functioning well, violent (emotionally, verbally, sexually or economically) even if not physically violent, or that the relationship is OVER and they should move on. As long as the person is getting their needs met - whether sexual, or the need to be in a dysfunctional situation - they will deny it's over. Yet when it really is over, they are the first ones to say, "Every one told me our relationship was doomed," or, "I should have left 6 months earlier."

Anger Management perpetrators are always sure they can handle their tempers and are in denial of their true anger and rage. Rage is anger out of control.

NOTE: WHEN WE ARE BUSY DENYING, WE DON'T HAVE TIME TO WORK ON OUR ISSUES AND WE AVOID SEEING THE ISSUES THAT NEED TO BE WORKED ON. No growth at that point!

The **ANGER** stage is ultimately what brings me most of our clients by way of court. Blame, accusations, arguing over little things that take them away from the REAL issues in the relationship or in the way they handle confrontation. When you are mad, you don't think clearly. No place for growth here!

BARGAINING is next, when the couple starts to offer options, like: "you can go bowling 2 nights a month, and I will go out with my friends 2 nights a month", lighting a few extra candles at church, bargaining with God to bring the relationship back to a comfortable spot. Again, not a time of clear thinking and positive work on the relationship, or on personal issues, just busy looking at options, diversions.

But, when we get to **DEPRESSION**, and all seems lost, when every avenue has been pursued - denial, fighting, trying options to save the relationship - then, and ONLY then, will **GOOD STUFF, good positive work,** start to happen! THEN the person will have to think about what has happened. Finally, let their feelings come out, deal with the reality of the situation. So Depression IS a good sign because now there is the chance the person will start to work on their issues and not just blame, deny and bargain! They will start looking at real options, and take some real action. Reading a self-help book, asking for help and guidance/counseling, recognizing something has to be done.

ACCEPTANCE does not mean someone embraces and loves the results, but does mean accepting the reality of the situation. In best-case scenarios, this is when the couple decides to separate and recognize they were not made for each other, and leave as friends. It's when the individual seeks help for the answers to the cause of their rage and anger. It's when each person in a relationship starts to own their own issues and what they "bring to the table". And the individual starts to finally hear what everyone has been telling them about their attitude and demeanor.

Bottom line - when we reach **Depression**, it really is a good sign, because it means it is now time to deal with reality and not stay clouded in Anger, Denial, and desperate attempts at Bargaining as we try to save an unhealthy situation, but now it is a time to GROW and MOVE ON.

When do you know you are successful? Or that you are successful with your clients?

True success is being able to spend your life in a way that makes you happy, that follows your passions, utilizes your skills and enhances those in relationships with you. And when things do go astray, the healthy person will take the situation under advisement with their inner self, recognize what went right, and what went wrong, then take responsibility for their own actions and consequences. In my practice, too often, I have had outwardly successful people reach an older age and then they ask, "Is that all there is?" They missed the personal growth, the love, affection, and impact others could have had on them, striving to make the "external" success show, while neglecting the inner person. Take time to look at yourself, where you are going and how you plan to get there. Make peace with yourself.

Becoming a good therapist means also **GETTING to KNOW YOU!** Don't rely on what others say, but figure yourself out BEFORE you are sitting in the therapists chair and working it out THROUGH your clients. You also don't want to be blindsided as clients say things that trigger your issues. KNOW YOU first the best you can. Of course, there will always be times when you will be caught off guard as clients say something that strikes home for you, BUT that should not be the norm. Look at yourself, your values, your thoughts.

Portrait of a Therapist

I can't give solutions to all of life's problems, doubts,
or fears. But I can listen to you,
and together we will search for answers.

I can't change your past with all its heartache and pain,
nor the future with its untold stories.
But I can be there now when you need me to guide and care.

I can't keep your feelings and heart from stumbling.
I can only offer my hand that you may grasp it
and not fall as you work through life.

Your joys, triumphs, successes, and happiness are not mine;
But I can share in your excitement.
Your decisions in life are not mine to make, nor to judge;
I can only support you, encourage you,
and help you when you ask.

I can't give you boundaries that I have determined for you,
But I can give you the room to change,
room to grow, room to be yourself.

I can't keep your heart from breaking and hurting,
But I can support you when you cry, or are sad and down,
and help you pick up the pieces, sort them out
and try to put them back in place.

I can't tell you who you are, or who you should be.
I can only listen, care, and let you become the best YOU.

J. Gordon
(adapted from Friend)

What kind of a person do you want to be?

The purpose of a life is to survive and achieve. We all want to survive and be nurtured in society. We also want to do well - to thrive, succeed, to grow. To do this, we need to possess three important qualities.

SELF-ESTEEM OR COURAGE

Courage allows an individual to try, fail, and try again, until they succeed. Knowing your strengths and weaknesses helps to understand your limits. Believing in yourself, you can learn whatever you need to learn. It is the foundation upon which the personality rests. We give ourselves and others confidence.

TAKING RESPONSIBILITY

We make decisions and choices and then must take responsibility for them. Some decisions can be life and death, success and failure: i.e., the choice to use drugs, have unprotected sex, suicide, drop out of school, quit your job, etc. If you have courage and self-confidence, you will make the right decisions and stand by them.

WORKING TOGETHER

In our society, competition is sometimes seen as "the road to success", in relationships, as well as in our jobs. However, the most successful use teamwork and cooperation. We are not totally dependent upon others, nor do we stand alone. In a society or relationship of equals, cooperation skills have high value.

So now, what kind of a person do you want to be? How do you want folks to remember you?

EXERCISES:

1. Write a 25 word eulogy here. Yes, it sounds macabre, but so often AFTER we die, folks say things they wish they had said to you. What would you like to say if you were writing about you?

2. What do you want out of life?

3. What personal (or life) values are most important to you?

4. What are some personality characteristics that make YOU who you are, that defines you?

5. Name three skills you feel you possess, things that come easy for you, talents you have:
     a.
     b.
     c.

6. What are three "roles" you now play in your life, and three roles you want to play? These can be permanent roles, passing roles, chosen roles, or roles you feel stuck with. Do any of them impact, enhance, or encumber your role as a therapist, counselor, social worker?
     Roles now:
     1.
     2.
     3.
     Roles you want:
     1.
     2.
     3.

7. Do your actions and life or lifestyle today reflect your values, personality and skills? Why or Why not?

8. Where are your present responsibilities in life?

As kids, we learned how to behave from watching their parents and other adults in their environment. The stereotypes we learn, we learn from adults. Kids feel they are expected to behave in a certain manner at all times, but they often see a double standard being established by the very people who preach to them "proper" ways to behave. It is no wonder kids, and us, as adults, later on, are often confused and get mixed messages.

A big step in working on yourself, understanding yourself and making changes is to understand and identify your feelings. These are the clues and cues to what is going on inside and what is in need of help or work.

What do I want for my life?

A simple and safe definition of Success - **To live your life in a way that makes <u>you</u> happy, but NOT at the expense of folks around you.** As we know from the television commercials and print ads, happy contented cows make great cheese and milk. In the commercial, we are shown how those cows hang out peacefully in the meadow and are able to ignore the flies and bugs, and not overreact because they ARE contented, at peace. You and I may not be cows, BUT we need to work on that simple wisdom.

What makes you happy? What makes you feel good about yourself? For complete understanding, you must know about the following, and define yourself:
1. Your values
2. Personality style
3. Skills, strengths and weaknesses
4. Roles you play in life and in relationships

VALUES

Values help people identify and express their core beliefs.

What we decide on and adopt as our "values" that we are most comfortable with; we reflect our own personal values. These are often things we learned as a kid, or just accepted and carried on as our own values. Sometimes they are values we adopt when we take on a new religion, move to a new part of the city, lose our job and have to downsize. Sometimes the values we have, or want, are not always clear. Clarifying and justifying values helps make you more secure, increases your confidence and self-esteem. The **introspection**, that often comes from growth in life, allows us to justify and solidify our personality and ideas, as well as our ideals. Values are usually what we care most about in life, and what we use to judge ourselves, our success.

EXERCISES:
1. What do you value most in life?

2. List personal values you feel you have now.

3. Do you stick by your values? Why/why not? What would it take to allow you to set your values aside? How will they influence your role as a therapist? Help? Hinder?

4. The best thing about me is:

5. I am glad everyone knows that I am:

Responsibility is often given as a personal value and a unit to measure us by others. For instance, "Susan is a very wonderful gal, so responsible!" Responsibility fulfills our needs, but how do we meet our needs and not deprive others of the ability to fulfill theirs? To the extreme, if a person is robbing a store to feed their children, they are fulfilling their responsibility to their children. However, they are depriving someone else.

Sometimes we get caught up in responsibilities to others, and become "co-dependent", meaning that we put others ahead of our own lives to the detriment of our health, wealth and self-esteem. It is good from time to time to inventory our responsibilities and values.

PERSONALITY: Aspects of you that make YOU what you are, and what people perceive as YOU.

Examples: Tactful, bold, sociable, thoughtful, energetic, funny, intelligent, stubborn, angry, close-minded.

• What are your major traits?

SKILLS AND APTITUDES: What comes easy for you? What are your talents?

Examples: Problem solving, working with people, working with your

81

hands, music, etc.
- Name three skills you feel you possess:

ROLES: These are different parts you play in your life; think of life as a script, what roles do you play? Most are temporary, and we change them as we feel the need. Some are permanent.

> Examples: "nurse", listener, "judge", little league coach, future therapist. We decide what roles we want to play and how.

- What are three roles you play in your life? Are they temporary or permanent roles?

- As a kid, I used to say the kind of adult I wanted to be:

We have spent time talking about values and responsibilities because they help define and set the pace for your personality. They are impacted by your skills, and the combination of all of the above defines the roles you play in life. Judging success is often elusive. Hopefully, as you worked through this exercise you got to know yourself better, challenged a few old values your mother told you that you had, purged responsibilities that cause you stress but no gain, recognized your skills, your partner's and kid's skills; and finally justified and clarified the roles you actually play in life. Often, we reach a point later in life and feel unappreciated for what we have accomplished, or what we think we could have accomplished. If we don't recognize and use our skills, take the proper responsibility, and follow through, much can be lost. Reflect and introspect, challenge your own values, justify them, fine-tune yourself, and be open to being the best person you can be.

SECTION IV
FEELINGS - DEALING WITH THEM

"Feelings, nothing more than feelings,
trying to forget my feelings.....
Feelings, wo wo wo,
feelings, wo wo wo..."
Albert

Feelings

Feelings. Scary topic, but we all have them, even though we may try to ignore them! Or, as quoted above, we write songs about them. When we say we feel "depressed" or "anxious", what we actually mean is a "state of being", usually a temporary condition, which can be broken down into specific identifiable feelings. We can identify those that are making us "feel" depressed or anxious. When we are **depressed**, we might be: sad, lonely, disappointed, hurt. Conversely, **anxiety** is the state of agitated, amplified flux. We have the power to work on the sadness, loneliness, hurt, and rid ourselves of depression and anxiety. Getting rid of depression and just be happy is a tall order, unattainable by wishing. By breaking down our feelings and identifying them, we have already begun "processing out" our issues of loneliness, sadness, and hurt.

Depression. We are emotionally overwhelmed by different feelings of sadness, hurt, fear, anger, and guilt. At some point, our mind says enough is enough, we go into a depressed state, stuffing and suppressing our feelings, a "rest" mode of inaction.

Anxiety. We are bombarded by other, different, feelings of fear, anger, apprehension, and insecurity. Our mind is agitated, unable to deal with the overall picture. Breaking anxiety down into specific feelings gives us a better "handle" at working things through, by processing out the individual issues. Identifying feelings is the start for most "processing out" in our lives. Learn to OWN your feelings, even those mom and dad, your teacher, or Sunday School teacher say, or said, you shouldn't feel! As humans we all should "feel" the gamut of feelings, even if for only a few seconds, from anger (which we were always told was a no-no) to jealously (definitely a no-no) to sadness, to boredom (not polite).

Learn to give a NAME to your feelings: they are, and can be, CLUES to what is going on, and CUES to what might happen. These CUES can keep violence and destruction out of your life. Learn to listen to yourself. Take the time to chart a week of feelings. At the end of the workbook there are extra "feelings" sheets for each family member, or you may print copies.

At the end of the day, check off the feelings you experienced. Use colored pens and pencils. On the first day, use a blue pen, second-red pen, third-black pen, etc. using a different pen or pencil for each day of the week. You will find yourself much more tuned into your life after few days of identifying these feelings.

Remember, your clients often cannot identify their feelings. You may say the classic shrink words, "How does that make you feel?" but get a programmed response, not a real response.

Therapist David Taylor used to respond in a unique way. When confronted with clients who would say, "I don't know", David's next thing would be, "Well, if you DID know, how do you think you feel?" That trick often elicits a response, as it takes the person a bit outside of themselves and they can be a somewhat objective. Remember, feelings can be scary.

With little children, I often tell parents that they have to help the kids understand what their feelings are. For instance when the two-year-old brother takes a toy from the 4-year old, and the 4-year-old belts him, just yelling "don't you dare hit your brother", is not the answer. Take the time to sit with the 4-year-old, and remind them you know they were angry, mad and annoyed at the little one, but that those feelings don't require hitting.

> We've bought into the idea that education is about training and "success", defined monetarily, rather than learning to think critically and to challenge. We should not forget that the true purpose of education is to make minds, not careers. A culture that does not grasp the vital interplay between morality and power, which mistakes management techniques for wisdom, which fails to understand that the measure of a civilization is its compassion, not its speed or ability to consume, condemns itself to death.
>
> — CHRIS HEDGES

- Feelings Chart -

accepted	frustrated	pleased
affectionate	furious	pressured
afraid	glum	protective
aloof	good	puzzled
ambitious	guilty	reactive
angry	happy	reflective
annoyed	hate	rejected
arrogant	helpless	relieved
ashamed	high	remorseful
bashful	hopeful	resentful
bewildered	horrified	restless
bitter	hostile	sad
bored	humble	scared
brave	humiliated	secure
calm	hurt	sensual
compassionate	inadequate	sentimental
concerned	inhibited	sexy
confident	insecure	shy
confused	intense	silly
defeated	intimidated	stagnant
defensive	irritable	strong
depressed	jazzed	stubborn
desperate	jealous	subdued
detached	joyful	sympathetic
disappointed	lonely	tender
disgusted	loving	tense
disinterested	lust	terrified
disturbed	manic	tight
eager	mean	tired
edgy	miserable	trapped
elated	needed	traumatized
embarrassed	neglected	ugly
enthusiastic	nervous	understanding
envious	nostalgic	uneasy
ecstatic	numb	unlovable
empathetic	pained	uptight
excited	passionate	vulnerable
fearful	peaceful	warm
foolish	pessimistic	weak
forgiving	playful	worried

Sharing Feelings

Silence is great amongst friends, good friends will understand. But, silence can also lead to misperceptions when we remain silent, and people try to interpret what we mean. They will put labels on us that may not be accurate as they "read" our actions. For example, our pet dog does not speak words. When it is not acting like it normally does, we try to "read" into its actions what is wrong. Does it have a tummy ache? Does it have something stuck in its ear? Is it just tired and cranky? WE have to interpret and that can lead to misperceptions.

It is important to get feelings "outside" of yourself, say them, share them, identify them, process them. As we identify our feelings, they become more tangible, less frightening, and not as much of an enemy to you. And other people start to get to really know you. Experiencing feelings is not always smooth, and usually more difficult for men than for women, and for boys than girls. Society often puts negative connotations on males showing or expressing any feelings that are not considered manly, i.e., anger is okay, insecurity isn't, strong is okay, embarrassed isn't.

Some people overreact as they learn to express their feelings, but as owning or identifying our feelings becomes more natural, there is no longer the need for them to be bigger than life.

Feelings give us CLUES to what is going on in our lives, LISTEN TO THEM, take their cues. Take possession of your feelings for at least 30 seconds! Be guilty for 30 seconds when you call in sick, have 30 seconds of embarrassment when you trip in a restaurant. Acknowledge the feelings. THEN process them out, get in touch with them by verbalizing them, talking about them, writing about them, talk, talk, talk. Time to share your feelings!

Getting the feelings out, processing them, is the key to a good working relationship that enhances your life rather than impacts it. That allows you both to grow not only closer, talking about them, but grow as individuals who are sharing a life together.

Some suggested outlets for processing feelings, both positive feelings and negative feelings....

...take a walk   ...meditate
...write a letter   ...do some yard work
...play music   ...pound a pillow
...listen to music   ...rip up some newspapers
...sing(loudly)   ...take a ride
...work out   ...call a family member
...call a friend   ...call another friend

**and...talk..talk..talk..talk
to your Therapist!**

Recognizing those feelings

As you explore your feelings, recognize that having feelings does not mean you need to act on them. For now, just recognize it. Your feelings are a part of you. Feelings hurt the most, and do the most damage, when they are denied. As you take possession of your feelings, understand that you don't have to deal with all of your feelings all of the time. They don't rule you, but are cues and signals -- to tell you something about yourself.

As you explore feelings, be comfortable knowing the value of identifying and expressing them.

-- Understanding my feelings makes me more honest with myself,
      letting me be more honest with others.
-- When I identify my feelings, I will be closer to other people.
-- When I know how I feel, I can ask for what I need.
-- When I experience feelings, I'm more alive.

EXERCISES:

1. List four reasons why you think it might be important to be able to identify and express feelings:

2. What are feelings? Define your idea of what feelings are:

89

3. How do you know you have them?

4. How do you express feelings?

5. How can you encourage your clients to express them?

Self-awareness: Understanding your Feelings
Understanding your feelings and their personal cues and clues are an essential part of your progress in life.

EXERCISES:
1. Name at least three feelings you have difficulty identifying in yourself. If you think you don't have feelings like that, remember these often are the ones, others may have pointed out to you!

2. Do you ever have a feeling you have a hard time communicating things to others?

3. What are feelings you find easy to talk about?

4. Would you like to change the way you handle your feelings? If so, in what would you change?

5. Have you ever been told you shouldn't feel a certain way?

6. What were the feelings you were told you shouldn't have?

There was a NEW buzz word way back in the 1970's - **COMMUNICATION**. Today with the internet and lightening quick interaction, we may not realize that communication was a problem. After centuries of anal-retentive, non-confrontive, co-dependent behavior, when people never told anyone how they felt, communication became fashionable. The pendulum swung, not to the middle, but too far. Often, people said more than they should have, or than was necessary, but this was "communication."

Now, we recognize the need for communication without having to hurt. We have found that stuffing, hiding, keeping it to yourself, putting "it" out of your mind, just escalates the anger and frustration. It lets stuff stay inside and percolate. Processing out the feelings is the key. Talking, writing, sharing are the best ways to process out feelings. But first we have to learn how to identify feelings.

> "The problem with communication... is the illusion that it has been accomplished."
> George Bernard Shaw

COMMUNICATING FEELINGS AND THOUGHTS

The expression of feelings makes a person vulnerable; it is an act of faith because it gives power to the person with whom one has chosen to communicate. However, once men begin to deal with their power issues in intimate relationships, sharing their feelings will be a part of that process. The expression of feelings is a sign of change. Sharing feelings is the ultimate in trust and intimacy in a relationship, allowing trust and confidence by the woman. Healthy expression of feelings is an important "new" skill to learn.

EXERCISES:
1. Give a few examples here of what you were told as a child and adolescent about showing feelings or talking seriously about what was going on with you:

91

2. List three barriers you tend to incorporate into your communication with others:

3. The time I don't like to talk is when...

> "Wisdom is the reward you get for a lifetime of listening
> when you'd have preferred to talk."
> Doug Larson

Forms of communication
1. Gestures
2. Tones of voice (How it is said)
3. Words (What is said)
4. Body language
5. Physical contact

Ways of communication
1. Passive
   2. Assertive
      3. Aggressive

• Describe yourself as Passive, Aggressive or Assertive, and how do you show it:

_____

You may misunderstand aggressive and assertive behavior. Many think loud aggressive, pushy behavior is a sign of strength. My way of explaining the differences to them is that passive is non-action, aggressive requires a reaction, and assertive makes a point but requires no action.

Aggressive action pushes a point at one, often causes a reaction in the other person to physically protect themselves, or emotionally to stand up for their honor, respect or values. Assertive action makes a statement that the other person can accept or not, but doesn't require a reaction. Here are some examples of ways of stating something:

Aggressive: "You must buy this product or you are an idiot."

Assertive: "This is a great product, I recommend it, you might want to try it."

Passive: "I think this could be a good product but I don't want to waste your time showing you."

Listening - Part of the Solution vs. Part of the Problem

We often jump to conclusions without REALLY listening or hearing. Sometimes we get ANGRY and attribute to malice what might be credited instead to cluelessness or stupidity. For instance, when a driver cuts us off on the freeway, the normal response is "why did that a'hole do that to me?" Sadly, or truly, it was probably NOT maliciously intended, the person likely did not plan on cutting you off when they got up at six in the morning, BUT were likely either talking on the cell phone, texting, or in another world and not even aware YOU existed. Also, not good for you ego, but better than thinking they just wanted to kill you. We've talked about constructive arguing, how each party needs equal time to express how they feel during an argument. But it is equally important to LISTEN! It seems odd, but listening can be more difficult to learn than talking.

Listening means "hearing" what the other person is saying, the verbal clues and cues as well as posturing. Hearing what someone else is saying takes practice concentrating on the other person. The person being listened to usually feels understood. Let them finish what they are saying, or make their point BEFORE you respond. Think, before you talk. What are they asking for - advice, support, validation?

How to Improve Listening Skills
1. Associate what is being said with a similar circumstance in your life.
2. Concentrate. Listen hard.

3. Don't be distracted.
4. Daydreams are no excuse for not listening.

Things that get in the Way of Communicating

1. Your expectations, especially expectations you've hidden behind before.
2. Looking for mistakes instead of successes.
3. Nobody's perfect.
4. Are you withholding trust?
5. Watch your language.
6. Open your mind.
7. Are you paying attention?
8. Fear of being exposed.
9. Secrecy!
10. Assuming.
11. Escalating Words like: should - always - never - why?

Being aware helps you overcome them. Recognizing "blocks" in others is ok, but concentrate on what you're doing.

What are three road blocks in your communication with others?

When I ask you to listen to me

When I ask you to listen to me
        and you start giving **advice,**
        you have not done what I asked.
When I ask you to listen to me
        and you begin to **tell me why I shouldn't feel**
        that way, you are trampling on my feelings.
When I ask you to listen to me
        and you feel **you have to do something** to solve
        my problem, you have failed me, strange as that may seem.

Listen! All I asked was that you **LISTEN,**
        not talk or do --- just hear me.
Advice is cheap: You can go online and get it free from Google.
And I can <u>do</u> for myself. I'm not helpless.
        Maybe discouraged and faltering, but not helpless.
When you do something for me that I can and need
        to do for myself, you contribute to my fear
        and my inadequacy.

But when you accept as a simple fact that I do
        feel what I feel, no matter how irrational,
        then I can quit trying to convince you and can
        get about the business of understanding what's
        behind this irrational feeling.
And when that's clear, the answers are
        obvious and I don't need advice.

Irrational feelings make sense when we understand
        what's behind them.
Perhaps that's why prayer and meditation work, sometimes, for some
        people --- because God is mute, and He/She doesn't
        give advice or try to fix things. "They" just listen
        and let you work it out for yourself, in Silence.

So please listen and just hear me. And, if you want to
        talk, wait a minute for your turn, and I'll listen to ... you.

ACTIVE LISTENING

Active listening is a way of listening and responding to another person that improves mutual understanding. Often when people talk to each other, they don't listen attentively. They are often distracted, half listening, half thinking about something else. When people are engaged in a conflict, they are often busy formulating a response to what is being said. They assume that they have heard what their opponent is saying many times before, so rather than paying attention; they focus on how they can respond to win the argument.

Active listening is a structured form of listening and responding that focuses the attention on the speaker. The listener must take care to attend to the speaker fully, and then repeats, in the listener's own words, what he or she thinks the speaker has said. The listener does not have to agree with the speaker - he or she must simply state what they think the speaker said. This enables the speaker to find out whether the listener really understood. If the listener did not, the speaker can explain some more.

Often, the listener is encouraged to interpret the speaker=s words in terms of feelings. Thus, instead of just repeating what happened, the active listener might add "I HEAR you saying, that you felt angry or frustrated or confused when ..." Then the speaker can go beyond confirming that the listener understood what happened, but can indicate that he or she also understood the speaker's psychological response to it.

Active listening has several benefits. First, it forces people to listen attentively to others. Second, it avoids misunderstandings, as people have to confirm that they do really understand what another person has said. Third, it tends to open people up, to get them to say more. When people are in conflict, they often contradict each other, denying the opponent's description of a situation. This tends to make people defensive, and they will either lash out, or withdraw and say nothing more. However, if they feel that their opponent is really attuned to their concerns and wants to listen, they are likely to explain in detail what they feel and why. If both parties to a conflict do this, the chances of being able to develop a solution to their mutual problem becomes much greater.

Active Listening Steps

Although the feedback step is at the heart of active listening, to be effective, each of the following steps must be taken:

- Look at the person, and suspend other things you are doing.
- Listen not merely to the words, but the feeling content.
- Be sincerely interested in what the other person is talking about.
- Restate what the person said.
- Ask clarification questions once in a while.
- Be aware of your own feelings and strong opinions.
- If you have to state your views, say them only after you have listened.
- These steps, are simple; however, becoming skilled in active listening requires considerable practice after the purpose and steps are thoroughly explained and examples are analyzed.

Performing the steps effectively depends on skill in giving appropriate feedback and sending appropriate verbal and non-verbal signals.

Verbal Signals

'I'm listening' cues	Statements of Support
Disclosures	Reflection/mirroring
Validating Statements	Statements

Non-Verbal Signals

Good eye contact	Silence
Facial expressions	Touching
Body language	

Most of us are occasionally guilty of sending messages that interfere with communication. So tune into what you are saying, and listen to what other are saying. Is there a congruence to words and body language for instance?

SECTION V
SAMPLING OF PERSONALITY DISORDERS

Co-Dependence (DSM 301.6 as Dependent Personality Disorder)

Typical Characteristics of CO-DEPENDENTS / CODA

* Assume responsibility for other's feelings and/or behaviors
* Feel overly responsible for other's feelings and/or behaviors
* Have difficulty identifying feelings--
            Am I Angry? Sad? Lonely? Happy?
* Have difficulty expressing and owning feelings–"I am feeling..
            Happy, Sad, Hurt, Joyful "
* Tend to fear and/or worry how others may respond to their feelings
* Are afraid of being hurt and/or rejected by others
* Are perfectionists and place too many expectations on themselves
* Have difficulty making decisions
* Tend to minimize, alter, or even deny the truth about how they feel
* Other people's actions and attitudes tend to determine how they
            respond/react
* Tend to put other peoples wants and needs, first
* Their fear of others feelings (anger) determines what they say and do
* Question or ignore their own values to connect with significant others/they
            value others opinions more than their own
* Their self esteem is bolstered by outer-other influences/they cannot
            acknowledge good things about themselves
* Their serenity and mental attention is determined by how others are
            feeling and/or behaving
* Tend to judge everything they do, think, or say harshly, by someone else's
            standards/nothing is done, said, or thought to be "good enough"
* Do not know or believe that being vulnerable and asking for help is both
            O.K. and normal
* Do not know that its O.K. to talk about problems outside of the family or
            that feelings exist and are OK/it is better to share them than to deny,
            minimalize or justify them.
* Are steadfastly loyal-even when the loyalty is unjustified and often even
            personally harmful
* Have to be "NEEDED" in order to have a relationship with others

AND...**the final clue to co-dependency is ... being willing to sacrifice your own/their own self respect and self esteem to accomplish a goal, even when it compromises your/their emotional health, physical health and wealth.**

Criteria for Depressive Personality Disorder (DSM 301.20)

A. A pervasive pattern of depressive cognitions and behaviors beginning by early adulthood and present in a variety of contexts, as indicated by five (or more) of the following:

usual mood is dominated by dejection, gloominess, cheerlessness, joylessness, unhappiness

self-concept centers around beliefs of inadequacy, worthlessness, and low self-esteem

is critical, blaming, and derogatory toward self

is brooding and given to worry

is negativistic, critical, and judgmental toward others

is pessimistic

is prone to feeling guilty or remorseful

B.   Does not occur exclusively during Major Depressive Episodes and is not better accounted for by Dysthymic Disorder.

Dysthymic Disorder (DSM 300.4)

Overview
Depressed Mood
Somatic or Sexual Dysfunction
Guilt or Obsession
Addiction
Anxious or Fearful or Dependent Personality
Dramatic or Erratic or Antisocial Personality
Diagnostic Criteria

Depressed mood for most of the day, for more days than not, as indicated either by subjective account or observation by others, for at least 2 years. Note: In children and adolescents, mood can be irritable and duration must be at least 1 year.

Presence, while depressed, of two (or more) of the following:
poor appetite or overeating
insomnia or hypersomnia
low energy or fatigue
low self-esteem
poor concentration or difficulty making decisions
feelings of hopelessness

During the 2-year period (1 year for children or adolescents) of the disturbance, the person has never been without the symptoms in Criteria A and B for more than 2 months at a time.

No Major Depressive Episode has been present during the first 2 years of the disturbance (1 year for children and adolescents); i.e., the disturbance is not better accounted for by chronic Major Depressive Disorder, or Major Depressive Disorder, In Partial Remission. Note: There may have been a previous Major Depressive Episode provided there was a full remission (no significant signs or symptoms for 2 months) before development of the Dysthymic Disorder. In addition, after the initial 2 years (1 year in children or adolescents) of Dysthymic Disorder, there may be superimposed episodes of Major Depressive Disorder, in which case both diagnoses may be given when the criteria are met for a Major Depressive Episode.

There has never been a Manic Episode, a Mixed Episode, or a Hypomanic Episode, and criteria have never been met for Cyclothymic Disorder.

The disturbance does not occur exclusively during the course of a chronic Psychotic Disorder, such as Schizophrenia or Delusional Disorder.

The symptoms are not due to the direct physiological effects of a substance (e.g., a drug of abuse, a medication) or a general medical condition (e.g., hypothyroidism).

The symptoms cause clinically significant distress or impairment in social, occupational, or other important areas of functioning.

Narcissistic Personality (DSM 301.81)

Remember, every person may from time to time exhibit "tendencies" toward many of the diagnosable personalities in a psychology book, ONLY those folks who persistently exhibit the behaviors listed or noted in each diagnosis qualify, i.e., all people get depressed from time to time, but if the depression is long term AND there is NO recent trigger like the loss of a partner/spouse/lover, then the diagnosis of depression can be made.

Narcissists are characterized by a pervasive pattern of grandiosity -in fantasy (talk of grand exploits or future immense wealth) or behavior (arrogant, haughty "airs" around friends and others), a marked lack of empathy, and hypersensitivity to the evaluation of others. In romantic relationships, the partner is often treated as an object to be used to bolster the person's self-esteem, a trophy.

It shows itself in early adulthood, and can be present in a variety of contexts, as indicated by having at least FIVE of the following:
1. Over reacts to criticism, usually with feelings of rage, shame, or humiliation, even if not expressed at the time but held within.
2. Is interpersonally exploitive: takes advantage of others to achieve his or her own ends. Uses friends, lovers, to get what they want, or to look good, versus being with someone they love and want to just share time with.
3. Is preoccupied with feelings of envy of what others have, and these are things they often feel they "deserve" or are entitled to instead of the others having them. "That car should be mine, not that idiots, I've paid my dues in life " At 22 years of age, saying, "Its about time my career got some where, I've paid my dues and deserve this NOW!"
4. Has a grandiose sense of self-importance, exaggerates achievements and talents, expects to be noticed as "special" without appropriate achievement. May use frequent cell phone or text use, as a tool to point out this importance often loudly in restaurants, and other public places.
5. Is preoccupied with fantasies of unlimited success, power, brilliance, beauty, or ideal love. Needs on-going facelifts or bodybuilding to be okay. One or two cosmetic procedures

(braces to nose job to hair implants) are normal, above that it becomes diagnosable. Not satisfied to recognize "at my age, and experience I'm doing well" but instead talks of the millions of dollars and the Mercedes awaiting them soon. Goes through date after date, finding none meets their demands, expectations, nor is worthy of them.

6. Requires constant attention and admiration, keeps fishing for compliments. Will ask ongoing questions in a public setting for attention, not truly just to find out more information. Will have multiple beepers proving their importance (to themselves!), or will have to receive many cell phone calls in public to draw attention. Often will over dress for the occasion, i.e., Armani suit for Wednesday night bowling league, getting many comments about the great look! "Don't you think this script is the greatest you've ever read?", before you've even looked at it, very needy of attention and validation, based on much emptiness inside.

7. Lack of empathy, inability to recognize and experience how others feel, annoyed and surprised when someone seriously ill cancels a date. Can't understand or "feel" others problems, is usually annoyed at their deaf friend for "not listening".

8. Believes that their problems are totally unique, and can only be understood by other special people like themselves WHO then could understand, and collude, i.e., folks who finally find that the legal system is fallible, and are shocked, then have to tell everyone else like "they just discovered it" and everyone else was to stupid to notice. Or like no one else has ever experienced isolation, prejudice or unfair uneven treatment in life.

9. Has a sense of ENTITLEMENT. Unreasonable expectations of especially favorable treatment, assumes that they do not have to wait in line when others must do so. Walks to head of line "cuz' THEY are in a hurry", parks in a red zone "cuz' THEY are only gonna be a minute", assumes rules are for others to follow, not THEM. Then gets mad when parking patrol tickets them in the red zone, "I just went into Starbucks for coffee, don't you have a life other than to harass ME (poor little me)?"

PTSD - Post Traumatic Stress Disorder (DSM 309.81)

Every one has heard of PTSD, but what is it? Here are the diagnostic requirements. NO, it is not the immediate response to a trauma, a non-natural death, and accident where some one is a mess after seeing it. PTSD comes up LATER, reacting to those things at the time, and for a few months is normal!

PTSD

A. The person has been exposed to a traumatic event in which both of the following were present:
(1) the person experienced, witnessed, or was confronted with an event or events that involved actual or threatened death or serious injury, or a threat to the physical integrity of self or others
(2) the person's response involved intense fear, helplessness, or horror. Note: In children, this may be expressed instead by disorganized or agitated behavior

B. The traumatic event is persistently re-experienced in one (or more) of the following ways:
(1) recurrent and intrusive distressing recollections of the event, including images, thoughts, or perceptions. Note: In young children, repetitive play may occur in which themes or aspects of the trauma are expressed.
(2) recurrent distressing dreams of the event. Note: In children, there may be frightening dreams without recognizable content.
(3) acting or feeling as if the traumatic event were recurring (includes a sense of reliving the experience, illusions, hallucinations, and dissociative flashback episodes, including those that occur on awakening or when intoxicated). Note: In young children, trauma-specific reenactment may occur.
(4) intense psychological distress at exposure to internal or external cues that symbolize or resemble an aspect of the traumatic event
(5) physiological reactivity on exposure to internal or external cues that symbolize or resemble an aspect of the traumatic event

105

C. Persistent avoidance of stimuli associated with the trauma and numbing of general responsiveness (not present before the trauma), as indicated by three (or more) of the following:

    (1) efforts to avoid thoughts, feelings, or conversations associated with the trauma

    (2) efforts to avoid activities, places, or people that arouse recollections of the trauma

    (3) inability to recall an important aspect of the trauma

    (4) markedly diminished interest or participation in significant activities

    (5) feeling of detachment or estrangement from others

    (6) restricted range of affect (e.g., unable to have loving feelings)

    (7) sense of a foreshortened future (e.g., does not expect to have a career, marriage, children, or a normal life span)

D. Persistent symptoms of increased arousal (not present before the trauma), as indicated by two (or more) of the following:

    (1) difficulty falling or staying asleep

    (2) irritability or outbursts of anger

    (3) difficulty concentrating

    (4) hyper-vigilance

    (5) exaggerated startle response

E. Duration of the disturbance (symptoms in Criteria B, C, and D) is more than 1 month.

F. The disturbance causes clinically significant distress or impairment in social, occupational, or other important areas of functioning.

Therapeutic Approaches Commonly Used to Treat PTSD:

    Pharmacotherapy (medication) can reduce the anxiety, depression, and insomnia often experienced with PTSD, and in some cases, it may help relieve the distress and emotional numbness caused by trauma memories. Several kinds of antidepressant drugs have contributed to patient improvement in most (but not all) clinical trials, and some other classes of drugs have shown promise. At this time, no particular drug has emerged as a definitive treatment for PTSD. However, medication is clearly useful for symptom relief, which makes it possible for survivors to participate in psychotherapy.

Group treatment is often an ideal therapeutic setting because trauma survivors are able to share traumatic material within the safety, cohesion, and empathy provided by other survivors. As group members achieve greater understanding and resolution of their trauma, they often feel more confident and able to trust. As they discuss and share how they cope with trauma-related shame, guilt, rage, fear, doubt, and self-condemnation, they prepare themselves to focus on the present rather than the past. Telling one's story (the "trauma narrative") and directly facing the grief, anxiety, and guilt related to trauma enables many survivors to cope with their symptoms, memories, and other aspects of their lives.

Brief psychodynamic psychotherapy focuses on the emotional conflicts caused by the traumatic event, particularly as they relate to early life experiences. Through the retelling of the traumatic event to a calm, empathic, compassionate, and nonjudgmental therapist, the survivor achieves a greater sense of self-esteem, develops effective ways of thinking and coping, and learns to deal more successfully with intense emotions. The therapist helps the survivor identify current life situations that set off traumatic memories and worsen PTSD symptoms.

Generally, PTSD-specific-treatment is begun only when the survivor is safely removed from a crisis situation. For instance, if currently exposed to trauma (such as by ongoing domestic or community violence, abuse, or homelessness), severely depressed or suicidal, experiencing extreme panic or disorganized thinking, or in need of drug or alcohol detoxification, addressing these crisis problems becomes part of the first treatment phase.

The following intervention principles are common in most cases:
- Educating trauma survivors and their families about how persons get PTSD, how PTSD affects survivors and their loved ones, and other problems that commonly come along with PTSD symptoms. Understanding that PTSD is a medically recognized anxiety disorder that occurs in normal individuals under extremely stressful conditions is essential for effective treatment.
- Examining and resolving strong feelings such as anger, shame, or guilt, which are common among survivors of trauma
- Teaching the survivor to cope with post-traumatic memories,

reminders, reactions, and feelings without becoming overwhelmed or emotionally numb. Trauma memories usually do not go away entirely as a result of therapy, but become manageable with new coping skills.

Psychotherapeutic treatments include the following:
  Debriefing (i.e., crisis intervention)
  Cognitive Behavioral Therapy
  Group Psychotherapy
  Brief Psychodynamic Psychotherapy
  Eye movement desensitization and reprocessing (EMDR)
  Hypnotherapy

Debriefing sessions are usually conducted as soon after the event as possible. The session usually lasts about two hours. A debriefing session typically involves a discussion of the event, the person's reaction to it, and coping strategies. Debriefing sessions are commonly used to help rescue personnel, classmates of students who die in auto accidents or as a result of a violent attack (e.g., victims of random shootings), and survivors of terrorist attacks (e.g., bombings of public buildings).

Psychotherapy is generally necessary in the treatment of PTSD, whether it is conducted in individual therapy or in "survivor group" therapy. Survivor groups may be associated with or may refer group members to local community agencies that offer therapy and support for victims of rape, domestic violence, combat, natural disasters, and so on.

The goal of psychotherapy in the treatment of PTSD is to help the person address and manage painful memories until they no longer cause disabling symptoms. This begins after establishing a safe relationship between the client and therapist. The process involves gradually working through the traumatic event and the patient's reactions to it, validating the patient's experiences, repairing damage done to their identity, and dealing with loss.

Cognitive-behavioral therapy (CBT) involves working with cognitions to change emotions, thoughts, and behaviors. *Exposure therapy,* is one form of CBT unique to trauma treatment which uses careful, repeated, detailed imagining of the trauma (exposure) in a safe, controlled context, to help the survivor face and gain control of the fear and distress that was overwhelming in the trauma. In some cases, trauma memories or reminders can be confronted all at once ("flooding"). For other individuals or traumas it is preferable to work gradually up to the most severe trauma by using relaxation techniques and either starting with less upsetting life stresses or by taking the trauma one piece at a time ("desensitization").

Along with exposure, CBT for trauma includes learning skills for coping with anxiety (such as breathing retraining or biofeedback) and negative thoughts ("cognitive restructuring"), managing anger, preparing for stress reactions ("stress inoculation"), handling future trauma symptoms, as well as addressing urges to use alcohol or drugs when they occur ("relapse prevention"), and communicating and relating effectively with people ("social skills" or marital therapy).

Group treatment is often an ideal therapeutic setting because trauma survivors are able to risk sharing traumatic material with the safety, cohesion, and empathy provided by other survivors. As group members achieve greater understanding and resolution of their trauma, they often feel more confident and able to trust. As they discuss and share coping of trauma-related shame, guilt, rage, fear, doubt, and self-condemnation, they prepare themselves to focus on the present rather than the past. Telling one's story (the "trauma narrative") and directly facing the grief, anxiety, and guilt related to trauma enables many survivors to cope with their symptoms, memories, and other aspects of their lives.

Brief psychodynamic psychotherapy focuses on the emotional conflicts caused by the traumatic event, particularly as they relate to early life experiences. Through the retelling of the traumatic event to a calm, empathic, compassionate and non-judgmental therapist, the survivor achieves a greater sense of self-esteem, develops effective ways of thinking and coping, and more successfully deals with the intense emotions that emerge during therapy. The therapist helps the survivor identify current life situations that set off traumatic memories and worsen PTSD symptoms.

Diagnostic and Statistical Manual of MentalDisorders
...the infamous DSM! Your Bible!

Psychiatric Diagnoses are categorized by the Diagnostic and Statistical Manual of Mental Disorders. Better known as the DSM-IV-R, the manual is published by the American Psychiatric Association and covers all mental health disorders for both children and adults. DSM-V is being introduced now. The DSM is the "bible" for any professional who makes psychiatric diagnoses in the United States and many other countries. Much of the diagnostic information on these pages is gathered from the DSM IV-R.

The DSM IV-R is published by the American Psychiatric Association. Much of the information from the Psychiatric Disorders pages is summarized from the pages of this text. Should any questions arise concerning incongruencies or inaccurate information, you should always default to the DSM as the ultimate guide to mental disorders.

The DSM uses a multi-axial or multidimensional approach to diagnosing because rarely do other factors in a person's life not impact their mental health. It assesses five dimensions as described below:

Axis I: Clinical Syndromes

This is what we typically think of as the diagnosis (e.g., depression, schizophrenia, social phobia).

Axis II: Developmental Disorders and Personality Disorders

Developmental disorders include autism and mental retardation, disorders which are typically first evident in childhood.

Personality disorders are clinical syndromes which have a more long lasting symptoms and encompass the individual's way of interacting with the world. They include Paranoid, Antisocial, and Borderline Personality Disorders.

Axis III: Physical Conditions which play a role in the development, continuance, or exacerbation of Axis I and II Disorders

Physical conditions such as brain injury or HIV/AIDS that can result in symptoms of mental illness are included here.

Axis IV: Severity of Psycho-social Stressors

Events in a person's life, such as death of a loved one, starting a new job, college, unemployment, and even marriage can impact the disorders listed in Axis I and II. These events are both listed and rated for this axis.

Axis V: Highest Level of Functioning

On the final axis, the clinician rates the person's level of functioning both at the present time and the highest level within the previous year. This helps the clinician understand how the above four axes are affecting the person and what type of changes could be expected.

"Every man has his secret sorrows which the world knows not;
and often times, we call a man 'cold' when he is only sad."
Henry Wordsworth Longfellow

SECTION VI
OUR OWN ISSUES

Sadness

Let's look at childhood sadness that is still with us. YES, I said childhood sadness that is STILL with us, within us, that we carried for all these years. Sometimes looking at old photos of our childhood years, gives us a clue to how we felt then. Often, we see sad faces but they might have been the "norm" then, so they didn't seem wrong. Of course, many folks have had wonderful childhoods, but those who have issues now, often had problems as kids, whether they knew it at the time or not.

Adult Depression, Anxiety and even Violence often result from issues that haven't been resolved in our lives, feelings we carry that might have hurt us. One of the childhood issues that adds baggage to our lives, and pressures us greatly, is **sadness**. Unresolved sadness and mourning, often gets turned into frustration, depression and often, anger. Because we are human, and can't take care of things, make the sadness go away, make people love us and not hurt us, not be lonely, keep friends from moving, loved ones from dying, animals from running away, our faces from aging, or our hair from turning grey. These things all start out as sadness, but turn into other issues, as we find in our mortal state we cannot wave the magic wand and make things okay.

Sadness can be things that were said, or that occurred, or by what wasn't said or what didn't happen. Sadness can be for all of the times we had to move, from a parent never attending school events, or from never being told that we were loved or OK. So many things hide in the cloak of sadness, and for most of us, as adults, sadness scares us. Sadness is something that we can't control and that makes others around us uncomfortable. "Put a smile on that face young man", "Don't cry, everything will be fine." Maybe it will, but right now the pain is there!

Complete the following sentences:

As a child or teenager, I can remember feeling sad about (whether or not anyone else knew that you were unhappy):

Was there anybody(anything) there for you when you were sad? A person, animal, place? How?

114

Today, can you express sadness with tears? Are you afraid to cry?

Present (as in here and now) Sadness

Draw a picture in this space of your sadness. Your sadnesses can be from past and present experiences. Remember this is yours to look at, and not be judged. Only you will interpret the pictures or words. There is no right or wrong way to do this.

NOTE: Drawings can be very cathartic for us, allow us to vent feelings through color and texture, often showing things we can't put in words. Doodlings as we sit on the telephone, or wait in the doctors reception room, often give clearer pictures of our real thoughts than what we may say at the moment. Drawings can be an experience.

Success and Stress

Financial success, owning a nice home, having a good reputation in your field of work, and finding your soul-mate are all worthy goals. However, it is possible to have all those and still be unhappy because of depression, anxiety, or other symptoms that come from unresolved emotional issues. The level of emotional health is the filter through which the rest of our life experiences are perceived. I urge you to ask yourself this question: is there anything more worthy of your time and attention than your own emotional well-being?

Take a moment and think of any person who has achieved greatness, not someone who has inherited riches or won the lottery, but someone who has achieved his or her goal. How were they able to accomplish so much? Personal commitment, hard work, and perseverance undoubtedly played a great role. Some of you may think that success has more to do with having good luck or good genes. I encourage you to read the biographies of two or three of your favorite successful people.

Creating a Balanced Lifestyle

Life is a balance of many things, all defined by you and your family. Just as too much sun or too much ice cream is bad, too much of anything can be bad. Enjoy life and ALL the different things it has to offer.

EXERCISES:
1. How would you rate these in your life? Put them in order from #1 to 4.

Solid relationships	Rewarding work
Spiritual activities	Physical Recreation

2. Can you have a balanced lifestyle with just some of these components? Do you have a choice? Why do you, or do you not have a choice?

3. What changes would you have to make in your life to create a balanced lifestyle?

4.The most important things I do in my life are:

_____

Your own best friend - Yourself

YOU are your own best friend. When you realize that, it is easier to be a friend. We all want and need intimate, caring friendships that develop our personalities, but first, we must start with ourselves. Too many of us become our own worst enemy instead.

Our challenge is learning how to respect and care for ourselves, while respecting and caring for others. What makes it difficult, is how we've been misled at childhood about our bodies, sex, men and women, pressures of work, the lack of support from parents and the economic realities of our lives.

EXERCISES:

How do you define Friendship? What is similar in the therapeutic relationship you will have with your clients where in many ways you are a paid, objective friend, and in 'being a friend' to someone?

Are you embarrassed listening to another person say something personal or painful? Describe what you find embarrassing, and why. If you have problems listening to friends, how would you adjust to hearing patients/clients tell VERY personal things?l

Stress

"Stress is physical", when we're under stress, our bodies react with the 'fight-or-flight" response. Adrenalin, and other chemicals are pumped into the bloodstream. Breathing becomes shallow, muscles tense up and the body prepares for action.

Four factors bring about stress:

ENVIRONMENTAL
PHYSICAL
EMOTIONAL
MENTAL

Stress occurs when there is an imbalance in the above four "factors", or when critical needs are unmet. The two most common reactions to stress, both of which cause even more stress are: use of alcohol or drugs, and sexual dysfunction.

EXERCISES:

1. How do you define stress in your life?

2. Name two physical symptoms of stress:

3. Name two emotional or behavioral symptoms of stress:

4. What does it mean: "stress is beneficial"?

5. What does it mean: "stress is harmful"?

6. What does it mean: "stress is energy"?

7. What are the causes of stress in your life?

8. What are the three skills of managing stress?

9. As a therapist, how will you manage stress for your clients if you can't manage your own stress, so how ill YOU recognize your stress, manage it, AND keep from Burn-Out?

And remember, stress can also be <u>good</u> for you, so don't confuse challenge, which is the opportunity to change, as stress. There are some simple techniques for controlling stress. They include:

    1. Immediate stress reduction or quieting.
    2. Assess realistically what we can and cannot do about the stressful situation.
    3. Identify your "feeling" response to stress.
    4. Directly discuss the stressful situation and feelings with others.
    5. Change your expectations, so you can do what you can do, and let perfection take care of itself.

"Reality is the leading cause of stress for those in touch with it."
Jane Wagner

Stressful Events

Stress is usually caused by feelings of LOSS AND CHANGE.
- Look at your life to see what repeatedly causes you stress and change it.
- If you are stressed by a boss that you hate, try talking it out with him, get a transfer, or change jobs.
- If you hold your feelings in, start expressing them.
- If you find that being isolated causes you stress, find ways to increase your contact with people.
- Coordinate your time, so that you engage in work <u>and</u> play.

EXERCISE:
Here are some common stress creators. Look at this list, and rate on a scale of 1 to 5, how stressful you feel they are. Write the value next to them, that you give them.

1 = low stress, 3 = medium stress, 5 = high stress.

Problems with your employer	Separation or divorce
Problems with your co-workers	Arguments with partner
You've been promoted at work	Sexual problems
You've been laid off, or fired	Family reunion
A death in the family	Problems with your in-laws
Pregnancy or childbirth	Being sick or injured
Marriage	Money difficulties

Now, remember YOUR CLIENTS will have the same issues, so think things through for you before you have to deal with them with your clients. Of these stress inducing situations you just rated above, and how would you personally manage them, and how would you approach helping a client with an issue if you had not, for instance, gone through a divorce? How can you understand those issues, if you haven't had them? Is it possible? Some clients will actually ask you, 'have you ever broken up with someone?'.

• You might end up counseling at a hospital, how would you handle someone who is terminally ill? What do expect of yourself in this type of stressful situation?

120

When you were a kid, and your mom/dad talked about stress, what did you think they really meant? How did they act when they were stressed? Did they give you any pointers about how to deal with stress??? What were some of the pointers they gave you? Were the pointers any good?

• Write a few of those pointers here that you remember:

Remember, stress can be good, so don't panic. Just learn how to choreograph things differently when you are stressed or know you may become stressed, so that you have safer boundaries at the time. By safer, I mean wider boundaries, with more room for flexibility. For instance, if you know you will be in traffic on your way to a pressure-filled staff meeting, make sure you take the sanest, quietest route you can, have the car with the best air conditioning, choose a radio station, or take a selection of music tapes that soothe you.

All you can do is try to make a difficult situation less stressful. I consult once a month at a small hospital 300 miles from home, in the middle of the desert. During the hot months, I make sure I either fly, or since I can relax and meditate when I drive, I often rent a new car from AVIS so the pressure is off if the car breaks down in the heat. There is an 800 phone number for a easy replacement! I also select music and satellite radio that will relax me.

Part of the stress responsibility can be on you, to know yourself well enough to recognize those situations you listed in the exercises, and prepare yourself. If an in-law holiday meal is in the offing, and that usually stresses you, prepare. Talk with your mate about it, plan plenty of time for the journey, watch your alcohol intake (less chance of arguments), take a good book, think of someone at the event who you do like talking to, and think about what you can share with them to keep out of the fray.

Life without stress is impossible. So make the best of it.

Holidays

Holidays often bring out the most stress in us. It is often amplified by the alcohol that goes with celebrations. We all have different views and feelings, trepidations, excitement about approaching holidays.

Holidays usually mean freedom and relaxation. For many people, holidays can really mean "Holy Hell." Trapped, as we are, in our early childhood memories, we struggle home through crowded airports, snow and rain to find nothing has changed. The only difference is, we're seeing what always has been there, but now with adult eyes. Each family member assumes the same roles and the carnage begins. Your parents will always see you, and treat you, as a child, no matter how old you are. You will resent your older brother, or your younger sister the same as always. With all this, how can you enjoy the holidays?

One way is to recognize that you DO have the option not to go to the family get-together even if it is the thing "you're supposed to do, since they are family". You need to meet <u>your</u> needs at this point, not theirs. Secondly, if you are psyched-up and prepared, you can go, observe and not get tangled into their craziness. Be safe, have boundaries, watch yourself, enjoy watching their behavior. Think of the things you have learned, look at the power wheels, identify their power and control trips, learn something about human behavior, and come home healthy and relaxed. Happy Holidays!

SECTION VII
KNOW YOUR DREAMS &
FOLLOW YOUR PASSIONS

"Life is a cup to be FILLED...
not ... DRAINED."
Alexey Galetskiy

PASSION / CAREER

From my book, "9 Steps to a Better Life" (available on AMAZON):

Follow your passions, not the "shuddas" in your life. Don't do what your parents, or society says you should do, but what turns you on, what works for you. Create your own definition of yourself. My friend Aaron, in spite of being deaf follows his passion about acting. I have never heard him say a thing about the money he could make in acting, or the fame, or the adulation he might get for his performance. But what I've heard from him is - **Excitement**!

Excitement about a new part, or a type of character he hasn't played before, or a chance to stretch himself theatrically and emotionally. Talk about extremes and passion taking you over - one day I ran into Aaron after he had performed a show for a school that morning. I noticed his face looked funny around his eye and I asked him what happened. He said he tore a contact lens performing that morning and was surprised I could tell that the lens was torn. I said, "No, I can't see the torn contact lens Aaron, but you do have a black eye." Since this was a show with all deaf actors, and he was signing the story, which was very intense, he had gotten so impassioned in his role, that he accidentally hit himself in the face and gave himself a black eye. While signing his part! That is passion for your craft.

Here's another point I think about, when someone takes the dirt nap, kicks the bucket, i.e, DIES, and it's time to write an obituary, you usually see that person described as someone who worked for 20 years at K-Mart, lived 30 years in Pismo Beach, California, and was married 28 years, etc. Instead the obituary could say something like, "He was known to roar through the Malibu Mountains in his sports car, while listening to rock music loudly playing on his car stereo. He lived at the beach, and surfed 'til he dropped. He was a painter of colorful intense scenes, full of life and expression." Now, you know a bit about this person, his passion, his personality. You get a "feel" for the person.

So, identify *your* passions. Follow those passions, let people know who *you* are. Respect the passion in your life. You need to know your passions. The things that excite you, turn you on, move you. There is nothing worse than having a boring unexciting passionless life because you are so dependent and insecure that you neglect your own needs, ignore your own passions and feeling, and blunt your desires, while blandly doing what others say you should do. Yes, in doing so, you might be politically correct and not offend anyone, but oh so boring. You'd cheat yourself, and those around you who might gain from getting to know the real you.

What if Elvis had ignored his passion for singing and been a competent banker instead? Or if Grandma Moses had been content to bake pies for her grandkids and ignored her passion for painting while she sat around waiting to die? What if Martin Luther King, Jr. had ignored his passion for equality and accepted the racial standards of his day? If they had, and many others like them, we all would have lost out. I recommend MLK's "I have a Dream" speech as inspiration.

You have to have stuff in your life that makes you happy too - stuff that brings the best out of you and your personality. Do the things that get you excited and thrilled. Share them with others. Enjoy them yourself. Everyone should have passion about something, whether it's flying, traveling, massage, sex, driving, dancing. Define those passions, find your passions.... because YOUR passions actually define YOU.

And if you have the passion for HELPING folks, GO FOR IT!

On your Journey to Self, **which you have to do before you become a good therapist**, and remember that journey is on-going, take the time to Learn something new, observe something new, every day.

Wonderment is a wonderful thing!

Build skills. Do things you do very well, keep an ego file of awards and commendations for those bad days. Appreciate what you do well.

Change yourself. If something you do bothers you, or your friends point out something they find irritating, consider working on those issues (i.e. attitude, tone of voice). If you can't change those things realistically or practically (i.e. height, ethnicity, quality of voice), stop beating yourself up over them, and emphasis your other qualities instead.

Never give up. A recent ad campaign included the phrase, "There is plenty of time to rest when you are DEAD." The only thing that really stands between mediocrity, giving in and excellence, between failure and success, is the little voice inside you that says, "I can do it."

Look good, feel good, take care of yourself. Low self-esteem sometimes begins with dissatisfaction about appearance. Look your best as often as you can - **your** best - not some unrealistic model in a magazine.

Physical Fitness. Exercise enhances feelings of positive well-being and zest. Be active, walk, run, swim. Don't be part of what I call the pre-dead, those who have reached the epitome of mediocrity and are stuck there for the rest of their lives, whether that is 10,40 or 60 more years.

Use Positive self talk, treat yourself kindly. Don't get stuck on your mistakes,"I did it again, I always do that, I guess I always will..." Instead, promise yourself next time, or next life, you will do better.

Be realistic, set goals realistic enough to be attainable, yet difficult enough to be a challenge. Set incremental goals for big project, each being attainable, culminating in the big goal.

Keep your perspective, mistakes are not catastrophes. Acknowledge your shortcomings, but remember you can never be a failure as long as you've given it your best effort.

Finally, as quoted in the first part of the book - take risks, expand the boundaries, try new things. "Been there, done that" doesn't mean you are part of the pre-dead waiting for the end, but rather "Been, there, done that, what's next?"

We are all a little weird and
Life's a little weird,
And when we find someone whose
Weirdness is compatible with ours,
We join up with them and fall in
Mutual weirdness and call it Love.
--Dr. Seuss

SECTION VIII
GETTING TO KNOW YOUR CLIENT

The following is the inventory I use in my office, I keep one of these in the file of most of my individual clients. Normally, I just use it as a reference when needed. Many therapists want to do a thorough inventory before they work with anybody. I know there is good and bad to that. I don't want to put the client off by making too much work and tasks in therapy which can happen with a two hour session to do the Inventory. And when you are doing the Inventory, it can come across as stilted to many clients. You are reading a script, and they may miss getting to see the real you in action. However, there are MANY things on here that you might not think of asking in routine work, and that have significant, often very significant, connection with where your client is!

I mostly let the clients work on what they feel they want to work on, I direct them around to the issues that I perceive to be affecting them, but when things get slow, I pull out this form and use it to get some further insight for me, and well as for the client, into where they are. To get to know them.

It's not a bad idea for you as you go through this course, to fill this out and get to know YOU better!

Beverly Hills Counseling INTERVIEW – INVENTORY

Name:
Today's Date:
(Please make every effort not to leave any blank spaces)

I was born in   on   /   /   at   am/pm.
When I was born, the delivery was:
I grew up in the city of:
My parents had child(ren), and I was number:
The names of my older brothers and sisters (in order) were:

The names of my younger brothers and sisters were:

Health problems I had:

Before I finished the 6th grade, I lived in _____ different places and attended _____ different schools. My mother worked outside the home, yes/no, after I was _____years old. She usually spent her spare time doing _____. I generally felt _____ about her work and spare time activities. She was always saying (or showing) that she was _____, and when I was with her, she would often seem _____.

My father worked _____ as a/an _____. (regularly, often, irregularly, not at all). He was often home/not home, which made me feel_____.

My parents' marriage was _____. I think this was so because _____. I wish they _____. I think my mother (would/would not) agree with this last statement, and my father (would/would not) agree with this last statement.

I imagine my father felt _____ about my birth and my mother felt _____ about my birth. When things got tough, my mother _____ and my father_____. If I could have had anything I wanted from my father when I was a child,
I would have wanted_____. If I could have had anything I

131

wanted from my mother when I was a child, I would have wanted
_____.

When I didn't get what I wanted as a child, I _____.
Through most of my childhood, I felt closer to my _____.
When I was very young (about 4 to 7 years old), my life was filled with
_____. At that time, I can remember being afraid
of _____. Afterward, about the time I was in the 6th grade, I spent
my time with _____. (brothers, sisters, friends, etc.)
My favorite relative then was _____ because
_____.

Note: When filling out blanks, add "step" parents, sig. others, lover, change pronouns as needed.

What I liked best, then, was _____,
and I used to wish that _____. I now realize that
_____. As a child, I considered myself a/an
_____ person, and I tended to associate
with _____ people. My main philosophy about
people was that they _____. My father
would become disappointed in me when _____,
and he would _____.

When my mother was upset, I was supposed to:

The secret I decided not to reveal when I was a child was:

I _____ my name. My _____ nicknamed
me _____. Today I like being called _____
because it makes me feel like _____ person. When I was
little, my favorite fairy tale, story, hero(ine), movie or poem was
_____. This was about
_____ who _____.

When I was an adolescent, my favorite character in the movies, television or in a
book became _____.
I _____ like that character because _____.

My favorite song when I was a child was:
My favorite song now is:
My spouse /partner regards me as_____ and I feel s/he is

_____. I expect my Spouse/partner to
_____. I _____ discussed with
my (have/haven't) spouse/partner the fact that I am coming to see a counselor. I
believe that s/he would feel such counseling would really_____
for me.

I feel what is basically wrong with me is:
I sometimes go out of my way to feel bad about my:
I usually take out my feelings on _____ by
_____.

The thing I feel most guilty about is:

I am mostly bothered by:

If, by magic, I could change anything about myself, I would change:

What like best about myself is that:

What I like least about people with whom I am in relationship is:

For me heaven on earth would be:

My biggest problem now is:

My life would have been much better had I been born:

The greatest difficulty a counselor is likely to have with me is:

My feeling is that s/he will probably:

I've noticed that:

One of the ways I avoid changing, even when I want to change, is:

For me, I would consider it "risky" to:

My life slogan or motto – what I'd put on my sweatshirt so people
would know it was me coming down the street is:

On the back of that sweatshirt I would put:

My particular talent is:

For friends I tend to select people who:

If I were to list 5 words that describe my father, I would say he was:

If I were to list 5 words that describe my mother, I would say she was:

Out of those 10 words, the ones that also describe me are:

If I were to characterize my spouse/partner, I would say s/he was:

To best understand me, it is necessary to add or emphasize the following:
  About my parents, family and culture:

    About my childhood:

    About my adolescence:

    About my schooling and friends:

    About my occupation:

    About my hobbies and interests:

    About my faith, religion or philosophy:

134

About my problems, troubles and trauma:

About my aims, goals, aspirations:

About my adulthood and present situation:

What, in simple language, would you like to change about yourself?

What will you resist changing about yourself?

How are you keeping yourself from changing the way you want to right now?

How are you keeping yourself from changing the way you want to right now?

What did you learn, directly or indirectly (i.e., from observing life style, body language, attitude, etc.)
    from your MOTHER about:
        SEX AND PLEASURE:

        RELATIONSHIPS:

        MONEY AND POSSESSIONS:

        GROWING UP:

    From your father about:
        SEX AND PLEASURE:

        RELATIONSHIPS:

        MONEY AND POSSESSIONS:

        GROWING UP:

How old are you now? How old do you feel most of the time?

How many more years do you think you will live?

What will you have written on your tombstone - what do you want your epitaph to read?

What was your mother's main advice?

What was your father's main advice?

If all goes very badly, what will your life be like, and how will you be feeling 5 years from now?

If all goes very well, what will your life be like, and how will you be feeling 5 years from now?

APPENDIX

Eye Direction and What it Means?

When you are doing therapy, you can get some clues by eye movements. Try asking some friends some questions and check it out. There are articles that point out ways you can tell if some one is telling the truth, depending on the movements. This is all based on how someone accesses their thoughts. Here are the ways most folks do, and you can see if it works for you, and watch your friends and clients to see if it helps you help them.

Visual Accessing Cues

The following are how a "normally organized" right-handed person looks (from your viewpoint, looking at them) while they are accessing an answer to a question. And where they are "reaching" to get it.

1. Up and to the Left indicates they are using Visually Constructed Images (Vc).

So, if you asked someone to "Imagine a purple buffalo", this would be the direction their eyes moved in while thinking about the question as they "Visually Constructed" a purple buffalo in their mind.

2. Up and to the Right indicates they are using Visually Remembered Images (Vr) to answer you.

If you asked someone to "What color was the first house you lived in?", this would be the direction their eyes moved in while thinking about the question as they "Visually Remembered" the color of their childhood home.

3. To the Left indicates Auditorily Constructed (Ac).

If you asked someone to "Try and create the highest the sound of the pitch possible in your head", this would be the direction their eyes moved in while thinking about the question as they "Auditorily Constructed" and imagined, this sound that they have never heard of.

137

4. To the Right indicates using our Auditorily Remembered (Ar)function.

    If you asked someone to "Remember what their mother's voice sounds like ", this would be the direction their eyes moved in while thinking about the question as they "Auditorily Remembered " this sound.

5. Down and to the Left would indicates Feeling / Kinesthetic (F) function.

    If you asked someone to "Can you remember the smell of a campfire?", this would be the direction their eyes moved in while thinking about the question as they used recalled a smell, feeling, or taste.

6. Down and To the Right indicates Internal Dialog (Ai) is going on.

    This is the direction of someone eyes as they "talk to themselves".

For forensic folks who use it to indicate lying, this is how this might work checking if someone is telling you the truth, or if you are trying to get to reality with a client, you can watch to see what is real this way:

    Example: Let's say your child ask's you for a cookie, and you ask them "well, what did your mother say?" As they reply "Mom said... yes." they look to the left. This would indicate a made up answer as their eyes are showing a "constructed image or sound. Looking to the right would indicate a "remembered" voice or image, and thus would be telling the truth.

Final Notes
- Looking straight ahead or with eyes that are defocused/unmoving is also considered a sign of visual accessing.
- A typical left-handed person would have the opposite meanings for their eye-directions.

The Hour of The Wolf

On the hour of the wolf,
the dark hearts hin and the pure hearts quail,
and the questions still remain

At the hour of the wolf,
that which was immutable is insubstantial
and that which was smoke
and shadow responds to your touch,
and the questions become... insistent

Upon the hour of the wolf,
Hours last for minutes,
and minutes last for seconds,
and seconds last forever,
and there are questions

When it's the hour of the wolf,
You'll punish yourself, praise yourself.
You'll love and hate yourself.
Cry about what you did right,
rejoice about what you did wrong.
And you'll ask yourself who am I,
why am I, and what's the point.

After the hour of the wolf,
You'll know who you are, why you are,
and what the point is.

But you'll be alone
And alone,
you'll never recognize your answers.
And you'll never leave the hour of the wolf.
David Sibley

SUICIDE

Suicide is a difficult topic. I have included a couple of poems from parents who have lost their children. At one time, there was a wonderfulyl sensitive website called "1000 Deaths.com." It was created by parents of children who had committed suicide. It disappeared, but recently another more inclusive one has shown up: suicidememorialwall.com.

There is quote, "The person who commits suicide dies just once, but the folks they leave behind by 1000 times." Suicide is a touchy subject, I get in trouble because I suggest to counselors that if a patient or client comes in and says they are considering suicide, I suggest to them that it is an option but lets look at what has brought them to this point. My motivation is that if somebody is so depressed that they are considering suicide, they don't need me to immediately make them feel worse by lecturing them that they are a bad person for thinking about suicide, but they will rot in hell for doing this, that they are selfish bastard for what they are doing to everybody else, etc. My philosophy is they are in enough pain already, and I want them to talk. If I play the critical parent by telling them how bad they are, I feel they will shut down and maybe not return. Of course, my goal is that as they talk about how bad they feel, and tell how strong this option is to them at the moment, and as we talk about who'll be left behind, and what arrangements they've made, and who they are going to miss, that they will decide there is enough value to LIFE that they will decide on their own, that THEIR life is still worth living.

How you handle this situation of suicide will be based on you, your personal beliefs, your religious beliefs, and many other things. I just suggest that you consider the fact that the person is in pain and give them a chance to talk about and come to the conclusion themselves to LIVE.

Below are some of the poems from the old 1000Deaths website, very moving. The first one is from a Mom, who found it awkward when folks would avoid mentioning her child who had committed suicide, perhaps due to their own fear of suicide, not knowing how to handle suicide, not knowing how to handle her emotion and feelings or, feeling they didn't want to upset mom by bringing it up.

The second is more about a mom wondering what she could have said that would have made the person not want to die. Sad but reality.

Remembering

Go ahead and mention my loved one,
The one who died, you know.
Don't worry about hurting me further.
The depth of my pain doesn't show.

Don't worry about making me cry
I'm already crying inside.
Help me to heal by releasing
The tears that I try to hide.

I'm hurt when you just keep silent,
Pretending they didn't exist,
I'd rather you mention my loved one
Knowing that they have been missed.

You asked me how I was doing
I say "pretty good" or "fine"
But healing is something ongoing
I feel it will take a lifetime.
by Elizabeth Dent

My Wish

If tears could build a stairway,
and memories were a lane,
I would walk right up to heaven
to bring you home again.
No farewell words were spoken,
no time to say good-bye,
You were gone before I knew it,
and only God knows why.
My heart still aches in sadness
And secret tears still flow,
What it means to lose you,
no one will ever know.

If I could have a lifetime wish,
a dream that would come true.
I would wish with all my heart,
for yesterday and you.
A thousand words can't bring you back,
I know because I've tried.
Neither will a million tears,
I know because I've cried.
You left behind our broken hearts,
and happy memories too.
I never wanted memories,
I only wanted you!

MONSTERS

The following story was written by a client who had reached her 30th birthday, she was very talented, but childlike in her behavior. In counseling, she finally approached the subject of her father's sexual abuse from the time she was nine. It had been a taboo subject. Mom and Dad told her that she had had the perfect childhood. When she ran away at 12, the police officer brought her home and made her confront her dad with the "vile things" she was spewing about this man who the officer knew as the deacon of the his church and to being a god-fearing, and loyal member of the community.

A month after she started opening up about the abuse, she was dead. Suicide. Read the following unedited story that she left behind, and see what you might find in the story that she wrote about 5 years before her end by suicide at 33. Clues?

"I feel I must warn you: what you are about to see is absolutely terrifying. When you turn the page, you will be tempted to slam this book shut and never, ever open it again. But please try to be brave. It is important that you learn the truth.

Please do not be afraid! I know the very sight of me makes you want to run screaming from the room. One look at my gruesome, ogrish face and my fiendishly sharp claws has caused many a grown man to faint dead away. I cannot help it— you see, I am a monster.

Sometimes, late at night, you hear noises. Monster noises. People may tell you it's your imagination, but you are right—it's definitely monsters, trying very hard not to crunch so loud. Please don't tell anyone.

Monsters are not messy, as certain fairy tales would have you believe. We always clean up after ourselves, despite the very real danger of slipping down the drain. Show this picture to an adult. Tell them how responsible we are, and how brave, and tidy, and how we make polite and thoughtful house guests. Perhaps they will want to invite us to tea. Contrary to our image, monsters are in no way mean or grumpy. We go out on a limb to make friends, and we are willing to bend over backwards to make others feel at home.

Yet, no matter how hard we try, people still don't like us. I've read all the story

143

books, and they never have anything nice to say about monsters. The pictures people draw of us, even scare us!

One day I decided to get to the bottom of this. I studied very hard, and I discovered an important secret. I will tell you, but you have to promise not to tell anyone.

A long time ago, before the fairies left the world forever, they called all the animals together so they could give each one a gift. The animals lined up eagerly, as the fairies gave tigers their stripes and birds their feathers. Humans and monsters were best friends, and waited patiently together at the end of the line.

It was sunset when the fairies finally reached them. Because humans had been so patient, the fairies rewarded them with the greatest gift of all: imagination. Immediately the humans began dreaming of faraway places. They forgot about the monsters and sailed away.

Because we monsters are so small, the fairies forgot about us until all the gifts had been given away, and they had nothing left to give but a small sack of magic fairy dust.

The fairies realized that it would be too dangerous for magic and imagination to exist at the same time. If humans got a hold of the magic fairy dust, they could sprinkle it on their imagination and their dreams would come to life. This would bring no end to trouble upon the fairies.

So, to keep us from sharing the fairy dust with you, the fairies put us to sleep during the day, and we could only wake up after everyone else has gone to sleep. The fairies also put terrible ideas about us into your imaginations, so you would never want to get close to a monster again.

But when we woke up, we missed humans. So we spilled fairy dust on the ocean shore, hoping it would lead you back to us.

We lit up the sky, so you could see us at night and remember us.

We painted the fireflies to remind you of us. But still you do not remember.

Every night we tap on your window to see if you want to play. But you hear only moths, tapping their wings against the windowpane.

We sing songs, but you hear only the wind, whistling through the tree branches.

In the morning, just before the sun rises, we must fly away to our secret place
Where we tuck each other into bed and tell scary people-stories. I used to be afraid of people. But now that I know the truth, I am not so scared anymore.

Look up at the sky at night. Perhaps you will see the path we made for you. It leads to our secret place, where we are saving the last of the fairy dust for you.

We hope someday you will come back."

GLOSSARY

Please note that thanks to the Internet and immediate access to the resources available today, a glossary does not seem as pertinent anymore to a book. However I will include a few topics in terms for your perusal that we have either discussed, or should have, thus they are HERE! And they certainly are terms you should be familiar with to go into the field.

Anxiety: an unpleasant feeling of fear and/or apprehension accompanied by physiological changes such as fast pulse, quick breathing, sweating, flushness this, aches and pains, or upset stomach.

Borderline Personality Disorder: characteristics include unstable interpersonal relationships and rapid mood changes in a short period of time. Behavior is often a radical, unpredictable, and impulsive within areas such as spending, eating, sex, or gambling. Emotional relationships tend to be intense, with individuals becoming easily angry or disappointed in that relationship which then is often short-lived. Borderlines tend to go to extremes in job and relationships as far as attitude and excitement.

Compulsion: uncontrollable, repetitive, and unwanted urge to perform an act; serves as a defense against unacceptable ideas and desires, and failure to perform the act or success at it, leads to overt anxiety.

Delusions: beliefs are contrary to reality and are firmly held by the patient despite evidence that they are inaccurate and unreal.

Depression: an emotional state characterized by deep sadness, feelings of worthlessness, guilt, then withdraw from others. Self isolation. Symptoms often include sleep lack of sleep, excessive need for sleep, appetite for sexual desire changes, and a general loss of interest in activities. When it is not accompanied by manic episodes, it is usually referred to as Major Depression or a Unipolar Depression.

Generalized Anxiety Disorder: one of a group of anxiety disorders that is characterized by persistent pervasive state of tension. Physical symptoms often include a pounding heart, fast pulse and heavy breathing, sweating, muscle aches, and often an upset stomach. During periods of general anxiety disorder, the individuals may be easily distractible and fearful that something bad is going to happen any second.

Manic Episodes: individuals may demonstrate unfounded elation and excitement, super happiness, as indicated by making grandiose plans, being extremely talkative, usually distracted, and engaging in purposeless activity.

Narcissistic Personality Disorder: a pattern of self-importance; a need for admiration from others, displays a lack of empathy for others - all common characteristic of individuals with this disorder. Often, boasting or being pretentious and feeling that one is superior to others and deserves recognition - prominent characteristics.

Neurosis: a large group of disorders characterized by unrealistic anxiety, fears, or obsessions. They are contrasted with more severe psychotic disorders that disable the individual.

Obsession: pervasive and uncontrollable recurring thoughts that interfere with day-to-day functioning.

Obsessive Compulsive Disorder: persistent and uncontrollable thoughts or feelings in which individuals feel compelled to repeat behaviors again and again.

Personality Disorders: these are characterized by being inflexible, lasting many years or a lifetime, and include traits that make social or occupational functioning difficult.

Phobia: fear of a situation or object out of proportion to the danger of the situation or the threatening qualities of the object. Examples include fears of heights, rats, spiders.

Post-traumatic Stress Disorder, PTSD: extreme reactions to a highly stressful or traumatic event such as being raped, robbed, or assaulted define

PTSD. Resulting behaviors may include being easily startled, having recurring and current dreams or nightmares, or feeling estranged from or afraid of others.

Psychosis: a broad term used for severe mental disorders in which thinking and emotion are so impaired that individuals have lost contact with reality.

Schizophrenia: severe disturbances of thought, emotions, and behaviors, may be evident by observing disorganized speech and reports of delusions or hallucinations.

Sociopathy: also called antisocial personality, or psychopathic, this term refers to behavior which shows no regard for others, inability to form meaningful relationships, lack of responsibility for one's own actions.

Special Thanks to:

**Alexey, Aunt Lil, Camille,
Carol, Christy, Evelyn,
Fred, Georgia, Harriet,
Janette, Josiah, Matt,
Muff, Rod, Ross,
Ryan, Shirley,
and Valentin**

2013

Beverly Hills Counseling
BHCounseling.com

This chart shows at what age a child learns - good or bad - the things that influence our behaviors as adults. These behaviors can influence our careers, relationships, and personal lives. As adults, they can also help explain where actions or behaviors come from and give us a clue where to start working! Find the hang-up/issue in the right hand column, and look to the left to find should have been gotten, and when, and hope that with 'healthy parenting' NOW, that the need can be met and issue overcome.

> "Its not the face pace of life
> that bothers me,
> it's that abrupt stop at the End!!"
> Aunt Lil

Age	Messages needed for healthy growth	How the child receives the message	Appropriate ways to give child the message	Abusive behaviors, negative interaction	Immediate and long term results of ABUSE
0-6 mths	I like to hold you I will meet your physical needs I am glad you were born I am glad you are who you are I like you	Symbiosis with the caregiver Food Physical Stroking Talking Having an impact on their environment	Feed, fondle, hold, talk Try many solutions or options Don't just let the child cry Learn about babies Take breaks and get support	Absence of primary parent Ignoring physical needs Hovering/ smothering Spanking, pinching, slapping Genital contact other than for hygiene	Food issues Lack of self worth Sleep disturbances Suicidal feelings Self destructive behaviors
6-18 mths	I will give you attention- You don't have to earn it I will give you love without conditions I will let you explore I will let you make messes I will keep you safe	Moving around Getting into things Dropping things Self-feeding Making messes	Give strokes (love) Baby-proof the environment Protect from harm Give unconditional, positive remarks and attitudes	Restricting mobility Forcing toilet-training Spoonfeeding, force feeding Hitting, slapping, spanking Genital contact other than for hygiene	Fearful of new environments Bodily elimination disturbances Fear of adults/authorities Food issues

18-36 mths	I am not afraid of you growing up I am not afraid to tell you NO I am not afraid to set limits for you I will not let you control me I will help you know your feelings	Testing and opposing the parent Being negative Breaking symbiosis Being allowed to be "self-centered"	Begin toilet training Use cause and effect thinking Begin disciplining by consequence Use problem solving Teach child to say NO to you	Expecting too much Being inconsistent Physical punishment Failure to discipline Making the child a prince/princess Spanking, hitting, grabbing Genital contact other than for hygiene	Dependency - trapped in childhood Can't say NO to others Low self-esteem Doubts own reality Manipulative

| 3-6 yrs | I will take care of you
I like ALL your feelings
I will set limits for you
I will teach you to have your own power
I will teach you appropriate behavior | Asking questions
Inventing Monsters
Identifying differences with others
Being away from parents at times | Answer questions with reasons
Encourage problem solving
Allow fear and other feelings
Teach how to get strokes
Participate in fantasies
Let the child know what to expect | Teasing
Believing a child is rational, and expecting rational behavior
"Sexualizing" child behavior
"Saying "because I said so"
Punishment for sexual curiosity or masturbation
Bribing for desired behavior
Hitting, spanking, genital contact | Sexual shame
Fear of being afraid
Adopting "victim" or "perpetrator" stance
Fear of others
Fear of differences |

6-12 yrs	I will help you make friends I will listen to you when you disagree with me I will help you think about your own rules I will teach you how to be safe I will help you set your own limits I will not make you suffer to get attention	Arguing Achieving Having companions Joining Activities Relating outside the family	State rules and provide structure Discuss values Listen to child's reasons Encourage task completion Protect the child's privacy Behave appropriately in child's presence	Teasing and prying Failure to follow-through with child Physical harm/sexual contact Treating the child like an adult - have your adult needs met by child Being too rigid/lax Commenting on the child's changing body	Promiscuous sexual behavior Self-destructive behavior Isolation, unable to relate to peers Unable to form relationships Stealing Accident-prone

Age	Affirmations/Messages	Developmental Tasks	Parenting Tasks	Unhealthy Behaviors	Possible Consequences
12-18 yrs	You can be different from others It's OK to find out who you are and to change your mind about it You ARE a sexual person (message: it's normal to have sexual feelings) You belong in our family You are loved for who you are It is not OK for you to get hurt or to hurt yourself	Being contradictory Being part child part adult Recycling previous stages Parent being available but not controlling	Stick by your rules and values Offer protection Listen without judgement Offer guidance Get your own needs met	Using the teen for work, sex or emotional support Being too interested in the teen's body Over protection/no protection Physical harm/sexual contact No financial support	Suicide attempts Unable to relate sexually Unable to work or maintain financial stability Unable to form relationships Sexual crimes Adopting a rigid moral code
Adult	You deserve to have your needs met It's okay to feel young, childish like (retain the inner child to "grow") Your reality is valid You can tell the truth	Recognizing and mourning the losses in your own childhood Consistently seeking all the positive messages you were not given as a child	Give yourself support people Re-parent yourself Affirm yourself	Ignoring your needs Using addictions to meet needs Hurting yourself physically Isolating	Early death Disease Mental illness Repetition of family abuse Criminal abuse